10 Minute Histories

BATTLES

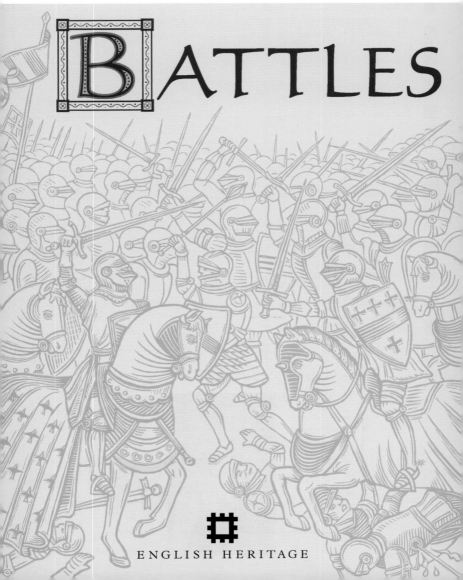

ENGLISH HERITAGE

Contents

Introduction

Arrows whizzing past your ear, cannons booming, bloodcurdling war cries and dead bodies beneath your feet – war is a noisy, messy business. Luckily, Britain hasn't had a battle fought on its soil for over 250 years, since the battle of Culloden (*see* pages 80–83). We're lucky to live in a war-free zone, unlike many other places in the world. But our lands haven't always been so peaceful...

Green and pleasant land

For over two thousand years, different peoples fought over Britain for money and power. England, in particular, was a prime target – it was seen as a land of plenty and much more of a hospitable place to live than Scotland, for example. To be the king of England was not only a great honour but also a powerful position to be in.

Invaders!

The mighty Romans, fearsome Vikings and clever Normans all saw England as theirs – a great place to conquer and settle in, and a good trading post to do business with the rest of Europe.

In-fighting

The reason for a battle didn't always come from across the Channel, though. British countrymen turned on each other time after time – sometimes for power, sometimes for money and sometimes for freedom. Many towns and villages were destroyed and thousands upon thousands of men were killed. It's hard to imagine people from the town next to where you live suddenly attacking you, but that's exactly the sort of thing that happened.

Everyday life

Battles didn't just mean killing and power struggles, though. The outcome of a fight could change the way normal people lived their lives too. For example, if the result of a battle meant that a new lord was in charge of your village, he might demand more money in taxes or ask you to build him a new house to live in. It doesn't sound fair, does it? That was the way some things were run in the past, though.

Read on...

In this book you can discover 16 amazing and bloody British battles for yourself. Find out about the weapons that were used, how the Normans won the battle of Hastings or watch **Lancastrians** and **Yorkists** turn on each other in the Wars of the Roses. You can learn why these battles started, who the main characters were, who won, who lost and who ended up in the Tower of London!

> **NOTE**
> Words in bold can be found in the glossary on pages 100–101. Where you see (**WW**) following someone's name, look in **Who's who** on pages 10–11 for a quick note about them.

Battlesites

Key

1 Maldon

2 Stamford Bridge

3 Hastings

4 Shrewsbury

5 Towton

6 Barnet

7 Tewkesbury

8 Bosworth

9 Edgehill

10 Marston Moor

11 Naseby

12 Worcester

13 Sedgemoor

14 Culloden

15 Bannockburn

16 Flodden

14 INVERNESS

15

STIRLING

GLASGOW EDINBURGH

16

10 YORK

5 2

LEEDS

MANCHESTER

NOTTINGHAM

4

BIRMINGHAM 8

ABERYSTWYTH 12 11 NORWICH

9

7

CARDIFF OXFORD 6 1

BRISTOL LONDON

13 SOUTHAMPTON 3

PLYMOUTH

Finding a site

Finding the exact spot where a battle was fought can be extremely difficult. Tracking down evidence that is buried under mounds of earth or modern roads and buildings can be a huge task. Teams of skilled historians and **archaeologists** can spend years finding such evidence, but when they do, what they discover can be amazing, from whole cannons to everyday items from battle camps, such as bowls and cups.

Soldiers marching at a re-enactment of the battle of Bosworth.

Bosworth

In January 2005 a team of archaeologists were given the exciting task of finding the exact site of the battle of Bosworth in Leicestershire. Most experts agree that the battle was fought near marshy ground south of Market Bosworth town. At least three different sites have been suggested for the actual spot where the battle took place, though. It's a real puzzle! So, using hi-tech computers and equipment, the archaeologists plan to rebuild the landscape of the time to help them find the answer. To find out more visit http://www.battlefieldstrust.com.

Bannockburn

The Culloden and Bannockburn battle sites have yet to be pinpointed exactly. In 2004 an archaeological dig at Bannockburn found some evidence that the battle might have taken place in the marshy valley of the Bannock Burn, behind where Bannockburn High School is now built. It's hard to be exact when so much time has passed and sometimes a best guess is all we have.

An archaeologist uses a metal detector to find the remains of a battlesite, such as musket shot or soldiers' helmets.

Who's who?

A quick guide to some of the important people in this book.

Bonnie Prince Charlie
Full name was Charles Edward Louis John Casimir Silvester Severino Maria Stuart! Tried to get the English throne but was finally defeated during the Jacobite Uprisings (*see* pages 74–83) and then fled to France.

Brihtnoth
Courageous Saxon Ealdormann of Essex, whose army fought at the battle of Maldon (*see* pages 14–17).

Charles I
Ruled Britain: 1625–1649. Not very tall – he's in the *Guinness Book of Records* for being the shortest king ever! Was tried and executed for high treason.

Charles II
Ruled Britain: 1649–1660. Popular and skilled king. Restored the monarchy to England. His arrival on the throne was celebrated all over the country because it signalled the end of Oliver Cromwell's harsh rule.

Cromwell, Oliver
Ruled Britain: 1653–1658 as **Lord Protector**. Was one of the principal commanders in the English Civil War (*see* pages 54–71) and, later, the most powerful man in England.

Cumberland, Duke of (William Augustus)
Son of King George II. Well educated. Famously ordered the slaughter of many of the wounded or prisoners at the battle of Culloden (*see* pages 80–83).

Edward II
Ruled Britain: 1307–1327. Completely ruined his father's efforts at conquering Scotland. Not a great businessman, he was unpopular and was finally murdered.

Edward III
Ruled England 1312–1377. Very successful king. Reigned for fifty years. Crowned king at the age of 14.

Edward IV
Ruled Britain:1461–1483. Born in France. Good leader. Capable and popular king. Tall, strong and handsome.

Edward V
Never crowned – was only king for a couple of months. Imprisoned with his younger brother, Richard, in the Tower of London by their uncle and was never seen again.

Edward, Prince of Wales
Son of King Henry VI and Queen Margaret. Murdered after the battle of Tewkesbury.

Fairfax, Sir Thomas
Very important Parliamentarian. Excellent commander-in-chief and general during the English Civil War. Nicknamed 'Black Tom' because of his dark skin.

Forkbeard, Svein
King of Denmark and the father of Cnut, who would later rule England.

Harald Hardrada
King of Norway. Well known for his fierceness, both as a king and a warrior.

Harold II
Ruled Britain: 1066. Before being king, he was the Earl of Wessex and one of the most powerful men in the land.

Harry Hotspur
Called Henry Percy but nicknamed 'Harry Hotspur' because of his hot-headed recklessness. Great warrior.

Henry IV
Ruled Britain: 1399–1413. Also called Henry Bolingbroke, due to where he was born – Bolingbroke Castle. Stole the throne from Richard II whilst Richard was abroad.

Henry V
Ruled Britain: 1413–1422. Henry IV's son. Famous as a skilled warrior. Very powerful king. Brilliant soldier. Shakespeare wrote a famous play about him. Buried in Westminster Abbey.

Henry VI
Ruled Britain: 1422–1461. Not well suited to being a leader. Deposed during the Wars of the Roses. Went mad.

Henry VII (Henry Tudor)
Ruled Britain: 1485–1509. Founder of the all-powerful Tudor dynasty which included many famous kings and queens. Successful and good king. Wise with money.

Henry VIII
Ruled Britain: 1509–1547. Had six wives. Very powerful monarch. Liked to gamble. Great sportsman, musician, author and poet. Established the Church of England.

Howard, Thomas
Skilled and respected commander. Under the title of 'Lieutenant General of the North', he was responsible for defending the north of England. Fought for Richard III at Bosworth and then changed sides to fight for the Tudors – not very trustworthy.

Ireton, Henry
General in the Parliamentarian army. Important commander in the battle of Naseby but was wounded, taken prisoner and managed to escape.

James II (James Stuart)
Ruled Britain: 1685–1688. Last Catholic king of England. Ruled Scotland and Ireland at the same time as England. After fleeing England in 1688, he lived in France.

James IV
Ruled Scotland: 1488–1513. Good king and cared whole-heartedly for his country. Invaded England twice – very cheeky!

MacDonald, Flora
Heroine in the Jacobite cause. Helped her sweetheart, Bonnie Prince Charlie, to escape after the battle of Culloden.

Margaret of Anjou
Henry VI's French wife. Important figure in the Wars of the Roses (see pages 34–51).

Monmouth, Duke of (James Scott)
Persuaded to try to take the throne from James II. When he was sentenced to death, the executioner took eight blows to cut off his head!

Norfolk, 3rd Duke of (John Mowbray)
Yorkist commander. Quite old at the time of the battle of Towton.

Prince Rupert
Dashing and daring. One of the most important Royalist commanders during the English Civil War. Was nicknamed 'The Mad Cavalier'.

Robert the Bruce
Famous Scottish hero who stood up to the might of the English and finally won the right to recognition as 'King of the Scots'.

Somerset, Duke of (Henry Beaufort)
Margaret of Anjou's chief battle commander at the battle of Towton.

Stanley, Lord Thomas
Clever and sneaky nobleman. Betrayed Richard III at the battle of Bosworth (see pages 48–51).

Tudor, Jasper
Well connected nobleman and Knight of the Garter. Henry VII's uncle and Henry VI's half-brother. Skilled military man.

Warwick, 16th Earl of (Richard Neville)
Nicknamed 'the Kingmaker' because he used his enormous riches and power to influence who should be on the English throne.

William, Duke of Normandy
Ruled Britain: 1066–1087 as William I. Also called William the Conqueror. Introduced many major changes to England. Built lots of castles, including the Tower of London.

Invaders from abroad

imagine foreign tribes invading your town, telling you what to do and expecting you to live by their rules. Well, that's exactly what happened to Britain time after time over 1,000 years ago, leading to terrible and bloody battles by the dozen.

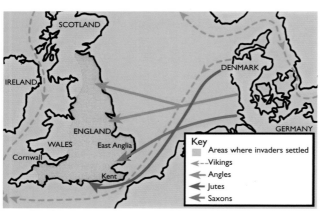

The routes of Anglo-Saxon and Viking invaders from Europe into England.

Invasion!

From the 5th to the later part of the 11th century, Britain was ruled by people called the Anglo-Saxons. Made up of three different tribes – the Angles, the Saxons and the Jutes – they had invaded Britain from Northern Germany, Holland and Denmark and claimed Britain for their own. How rude!

More unwanted guests

If the Anglo-Saxons weren't bad enough, next came the Vikings! They were also known as 'Norsemen' and sailed over from Norway, Sweden and Denmark. With their super-strength warriors, they attacked Britain again and again until, eventually, one of their vicious attacks paid off and they grabbed a whole chunk of land to live on.

The word Viking meant 'a pirate raid' in Old Norse – the Viking language

Keeping the peace

There were now many different peoples living in Britain, and despite dividing up the country, the different tribes were always fighting with one another.

Skills

The native Britons didn't appear to have much of a say in how things in Britain were run, but there were some benefits to these invasions from abroad. The Vikings were also great farmers and traders and spread their outstanding skills in these two areas everywhere they settled.

The Viking legacy

The Vikings, whilst best remembered for their ferocity in battle, were also brilliant shipbuilders. Their vessels were at the forefront of technology, enabling them to travel great distances. Viking ships were also very strong and could skim through water quickly.

The curved design of a Viking ship meant that it could sail right up onto a beach – handy for the Vikings to jump out and make a quick attack.

An Anglo-Saxon diary

The Anglo-Saxons also helped to shape Britain for the better. The Anglo-Saxon Chronicles is a collection of very important historical documents from the **Dark and Middle Ages**. They are a kind of diary, telling what life was like in Britain. This is a typical entry:

'A.D. 956. This year died Wulfstan, Archbishop of York, on the seventeenth day before the calends of January; and he was buried at Oundle;'

The Chronicles were written by nuns and monks. They were first started by King Alfred the Great in AD 890 and contain 1,000 years of history.

Language

Many words that we use every day are either Anglo-Saxon or Norse, such as 'father', 'daughter', 'son', 'cheese' and most of the names of our towns and villages.

The battle of Maldon

Date: 10 August 991
Where: Maldon, Essex
Why: money
Armies: Vikings vs. Saxons
Who won: Vikings

When a ferocious Viking army landed on the Isle of Northey, Essex, in the summer of 991, they had one thing on their mind – treasure! What better place to find such booty than in the nearby settlement of Maldon – home to one of the country's largest **mints**.

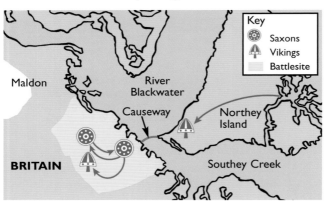

This map shows how the Viking army moved from Northey Island into mainland England, and then how the two sides moved once in battle

Brihtnoth takes up the fight

A Saxon **Ealdormann** called Brihtnoth (**WW**) was given the frightening task of seeing off the Viking soldiers led by Svein Forkbeard (**WW**). Despite having quite a small army, Brihtnoth bravely rose to the challenge, meeting the Vikings at a **causeway** which separated Northey from the mainland. Luckily, the tide was starting to rise, stopping the enemy from crossing the water. Whilst they waited for the tide to turn, the leaders of the two sides hurled insults at each other. Forkbeard demanded money in exchange for leaving England alone but Brihtnoth refused. Instead, he challenged the Viking invaders to a battle.

A statue of Brihtnoth sits above the entrance to All Saints Church, Maldon.

Daring tactics

As Forkbeard had such a large army, Brihtnoth needed to think carefully about his tactics. He knew that he would have a better chance of defeating the Vikings if they had to come onto the mainland by squeezing through the narrow causeway. So, he invited them over! Forkbeard became worried. He, too, saw that his army could easily be slain in the trip across the water, so, he politely asked Brihtnoth for fighting to start only once all his men were safely across. A Viking being polite – now that's something! Crazily, Brihtnoth agreed.

The Viking army is hungry for battle. They wait for the tide to turn and then head onto the mainland – and to battle!

Shields

Shields were an essential part of a soldier's kit. Saxon and Viking warriors didn't have much body armour to protect them, so they used their shields to guard against enemy attacks. Their shields were usually round and made from wood and leather. They also had straps attached so that they could be worn over the back, like a rucksack.

A wise decision

Brihtnoth's decision to let Forkbeard and his men across the causeway wasn't as stupid as it sounds. He wanted to force the Vikings into battle with him so that he could crush them completely, preventing raids on other towns along the British coastline.

A hearty drink before a battle was normal for Viking warriors – it was all part of rousing courage for the fight that lay ahead.

Into battle!

The fighting broke out immediately. Brihtnoth quickly ordered his army to overlap their shields to form a strong **shieldwall** and wait for the enemy to strike. The Vikings charged at the wall, smashing through it, and soon the two sides were engaged in brutal hand-to-hand combat.

🛡 The Viking warriors would have been a frightening force as they stood fast waiting to attack the Saxon army.

Brihtnoth falls

Brihtnoth was fighting on the frontline – a brave move for the leader of the army. Despite his valiant efforts, it wasn't long before he was struck by the enemy – first by a Viking spear, next by a javelin and then by a blade through his sword-arm. Finally, he sank to his knees as a final blow cut off his head.

Last stand

On seeing their leader killed, many Saxon soldiers lost confidence and ran for their lives, but Brihtnoth's loyal **hearth-troop** stayed to avenge him. So, even though the Vikings won the battle of Maldon and got the gold that they had come for, Brihtnoth's brave men made sure that they paid for it with many Danish lives. It was said at the time that, even though they were victorious, the Vikings had barely enough men to crew the ships on the voyage home.

🛡 Most soldiers would have been given spears to fight with but noblemen, like these, above, would have been equipped with swords – a most prized weapon.

🛡 Saxons load their catapult ready for firing at their enemy.

Brihtnoth's body

The Vikings stole Brihtnoth's severed head as a battle trophy but the monks of nearby Ely Cathedral recovered his body. He is still buried there, in the Bishop's West Chapel with a wax head instead of a real one.

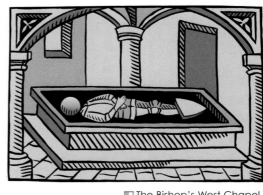

The Bishop's West Chapel is the resting place for six other Saxon noblemen who were also killed at the battle of Maldon.

A Viking king for Britain

The battle of Maldon was the first Saxon defeat that had happened in a long time. It led to more Viking raids until eventually, in 1016, Viking King Cnut claimed the English crown and became the first Viking king of England.

The Battle of Maldon

Old English

Þær wearo hream ahafen,
earn æses georn;
Hi leton pa of folman
gegrundene
bogan wæron bysige,
Biter wæs se beaduræs,
on gehwæoere hand,

hremmas wundon,
wæs on eorpan cyrm.
feolhearde speru,
garas fleogan;
bord ord onfeng.
beornas feollon
hyssas lagon.

A modern translation

Now was riot raised, the ravens wheeled,
The eagle, eager for carrion, there was a cry on earth.
Then loosed they from their hands the file-hard lance,
The sharp-ground spears to fly.
Bows were busied – buckler met point
Bitter was the battle-rush, warriors fell
On either hand, the young men lay!

A famous and very long poem was written for Brihtnoth's widow about the battle. It's the best account we have today to tell us what actually happened in Maldon all those years ago.

The battle of Stamford Bridge

Date: 25 September 1066
Where: Stamford Bridge, near York
Why: the right to the English throne
Armies: Vikings vs. Saxons
Who won: Saxons

The second most famous battle of 1066 happened near York just a few days before the most famous one of Hastings. It was a bloody battle fought between King Harold II (**WW**) and the fearsome King Harald Hardrada of Norway (**WW**).

Trouble arrives!

Hardrada arrived from Norway with about 300 ships full to bursting with war-hungry Vikings and a powerful ally – Harold II's brother, Tostig. With the help of Tostig's Scottish army the two of them started fighting in the north of England. They won their first battle near York and, with 100 terrified hostages in tow for security, they felt confident that they had a firm grip on northern England.

⬙ A Viking fleet in full sail would have been awesome to see – and very frightening if you weren't on their side!

⬙ An old map showing the site of the battle at Stamford Bridge.

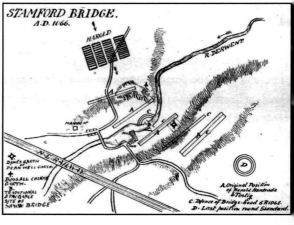

STAMFORD BRIDGE.
A.D. 1066.

HAROLD

R. DERWENT

A. Original Position of Harold Hardrada & Tostig
C. Defence of Bridge-head & RIDGE
D. Last position round Standard

A walk in the park

Confident of their victorious position, Hardrada and Tostig relaxed. They agreed to hand over their hostages to the king's men at a place called Stamford Bridge and, thinking they wouldn't need them, they sent most of the Viking men back to their ships.

The Saxon army gets ready for battle.

Surprise, surprise!

The small army that Hardrada had left marched south. Little did they know that King Harold and his troops were already sneakily waiting at Stamford, ready for battle. Hardrada must have done a double-take when he caught sight of the morning light bouncing off the enemies' spears! He panicked and immediately sent for reinforcements.

The insults fly

As they faced each other, ready for battle, the two leaders exchanged insults. Harold offered his brother, Tostig, the chance to save his skin and fight alongside him. Tostig refused – he was sure that the Vikings would win. Harold told Hardrada that the only piece of British soil he would get would be in the form of a grave. Brave words, indeed! But soon the time for talking was at an end – the only way to sort this out was in battle.

Helmet

Mail shirt: made from hundreds of iron rings

Dagger: good for close combat

Battle axe

Round Viking shield

Tunic

Sword

Vikings didn't wear helmets with horns, like you see in cartoons, but ones with protective eyepieces instead.

The battle

Harold's army attacked the Vikings with all their might. Despite the fact that the rest of their men hadn't yet arrived, Hardrada's men fought back bravely, stopping the Saxons from crossing the bridge at Stamford. Historical accounts tell us that one Viking warrior on the bridge was killed by some Saxons in a boat below him who stabbed his bottom with a spear. Poor chap!

The Vikings were heavily outnumbered but fought on with great courage.

Harald falls

Eventually, in a gory and exhausting battle that lasted all day, the Viking shieldwall fell. Hardrada was determined to fight to the end, however. In one desperate last stand, he took his sword in both hands and hacked through the Saxon army, only to be slain in his tracks by an arrow slicing through his windpipe.

The Swordsman Inn sits next to the battlesite. Its sign shows a scene from the battle.

Game over

With their king gone and their army reduced to just a small number, the disorganised Vikings didn't know what to do. Reinforcements finally arrived from the Viking ships but they were far too late and any Vikings that were left alive fled the battlefield.

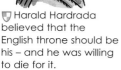

Harald Hardrada believed that the English throne should be his – and he was willing to die for it.

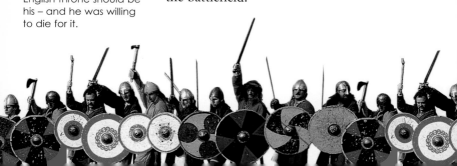

Viking weapons

The most common Viking weapons were spears, swords and battle axes. Their weapons weren't just for fighting, though. They also symbolised wealth and how important a warrior was within his tribe. Some weapons were ornately decorated with beautiful patterns or pieces of silver or bronze.

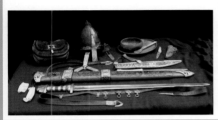

Swords were very expensive to make and, as such, only very important men would carry one. Viking craftsmen sometimes created highly decorated **hilts** and gave their swords names. This collection, left, is part of a typical kit including small knives, eating implements, a helmet and a storage bag.

The Stamford Bridge monument.

Losses

King Harold was true to his word and gave Hardrada his grave in the form of 'seven feet of English earth'. Tostig was also killed in the battle and is buried in York. We're not sure how many men died altogether during the battle but the Vikings would have lost many more soldiers than the Saxon army.

What's next?

This battle was an important victory for England. It marked the end of the Viking threat to the English throne and showed that Harold was a strong warrior. He didn't have the chance to feel safe for long, though; an even greater danger in the form of William of Normandy had arrived in Britain near a town called Hastings...

The battle of Hastings

Date: 14 October 1066
Where: Senlac Hill, Sussex
Why: the right to the English throne
Armies: English vs. a French allied army (Normans, Bretons & Flemish)
Who won: French allied army

On an October morning in Sussex in 1066, the armies of King Harold II and William Duke of Normandy (**WW**) fought one of the most important and famous struggles on English soil ever – the battle of Hastings.

🛡 William, Duke of Normandy, said that his cousin, King Edward, who was king before Harold II, had made him heir to the English throne.

Army numbers

William arrived in England from France with a 7,500-strong army, determined to fight for his right to the English throne. King Harold was completely exhausted by his efforts at Stamford Bridge but, without a second thought, he hurried south to meet William. He set up camp with an army of 8,000 men about 12 miles from Hastings.

🛡 Some shields – like these Norman ones – were kite-shaped. They were flat or curved and their length meant that they protected more of the soldier's body than a round shield did.

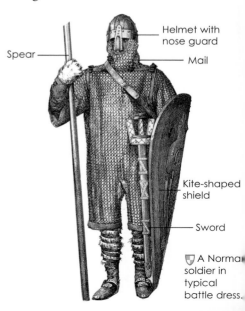

Spear

Helmet with nose guard

Mail

Kite-shaped shield

Sword

🛡 A Norman soldier in typical battle dress.

The battle

As the battle began, Harold positioned his army at the top of a steep hill called Senlac. His men made a deep heavy-duty shieldwall, which stretched for over 700 metres and would have seemed impossible to break through.

Harold's Saxon shieldwall forms to face the Norman attack.

The allies struggle

The allied French army at the bottom of the hill were weighed down by their heavy chain mail and weapons. This made it difficult for them to run up the hill and break through the tough wall of Saxon men above them. Some of the Norman army gave up and started to run back down the hill, knocking William from his horse. The horse was killed outright and rumours started to spread amongst the men – was William dead too...?

A Norman knight raises his sword – a sign that William is alive.

William fights back

Unluckily for Harold, the answer was no. William was very much alive – and ready to continue the fight! He quickly chucked a lowly Norman soldier off his horse, claimed it for his own and joined the raging battle once again.

The Bayeux Tapestry

The tapestry is a history book made of cloth over 70 m in length. It shows the events that happened in 1066 and still exists, 1,000 years after it was made, in Bayeux, Normandy. The pictures on the tapestry show 623 people, 202 horses and mules, 55 dogs, over 500 other animals, 37 buildings and 41 ships.

The chase is on!

But seeing that some of the enemy had started to flee, some of Harold's army thought that they had won the battle. They foolishly chased the retreating Norman army down Senlac hill.

The Norman cavalry prepare to charge.

Sneaky tricks

Halfway down the Normans turned on them and, despite trying to scramble back up the hill, the English soldiers were slaughtered. This weakened the strong English shieldwall and showed the Normans a clever way of using the hill to their advantage. They decided to repeat this sneaky trick a few times but Harold's special bodyguard (and the hardest men of the bunch) were wise to it and stayed put on top of the hill.

The Saxon shieldwall falls apart and the close fighting begins.

Blood and guts

By now both sides were feeling the strain – fighting on hills is tiring, to say the least. Many men had been killed and those that were left were aching and exhausted. The brutal hand-to-hand combat meant that the soldiers' shields and weapons were covered in blood and guts. What's more, the corpses and dismembered body parts had turned the ground into a gory, mushy mess.

Harold's fall

Finally, after nearly a whole day of fighting, William ordered his archers to attack. They did so and wounded Harold near his eye. In the turmoil that followed, Harold was left unprotected and William and some of his Norman knights rushed to finish him off. The English army were in total disorder at the loss of their king, making it easy for William's men to claim their victory.

🛡 You had to kill or be killed in battle and the defeated were often given "No quarter" (see page 37).

All change in England

The battle of Hastings saw the end of the Saxon reign and the beginning of the Norman **dynasty**. King William I ruled England for 19 years and brought many changes to life here. He had many important castles built, such as Battle Abbey, below, and the Tower of London. Norman French replaced English as the language spoken by the **nobility** for nearly 300 years and many words still exist in our language today. William was succeeded in 1087 by his younger son, William Rufus.

Domesday Book

In 1085 William ordered the first complete survey of England and all its people. It is called the Domesday Book.

The end of an age

William's invasion is seen as a turning point in English and European history and is used by many historians to signal the end of the Dark Ages and the beginning of the Middle Ages.

🛡 The battle of Hastings didn't actually take place at Hastings at all but 13 km away at a place now called Battle. The magnificent Battle Abbey now stands on the spot where Harold died.

Weapons

As warfare has developed over the years, fighting tools have become more and more sophisticated. The hi-tech weapons of today seem a far cry from those used a thousand years ago. At the battle of Sedgemoor, for example, some soldiers used pitchforks to fight with because they didn't have proper weapons.

Spear
Good for
slashing and stabbing your enemy through their shieldwall.

Sword
A sword was a prized weapon.
Medieval swords were made of steel with
a wooden handle and an iron crossguard.

Axe
Used for hand-to-hand fighting or thrown like a missile at the enemy.

Mace
A wood or steel club-like weapon that could kill or break bones, even through thick mail.

Longbow
The introduction of the longbow in the 12th century showed what a mighty weapon the bow could be. A longbow could be over 1.85 m long, and the arrows used were wooden with a deadly-sharp iron head. A good bowman could keep up to ten arrows in the air at any one time and hit a target 320 m away!

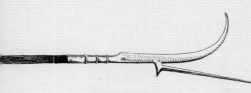

Bill

Also called a bill hook. Good for close combat. Over 1.8 m long with a chopping blade and other spikes at one end.

Pike

A type of long, pointed spear – sometimes up to 6 m long – with a nasty steel tip. Used by **infantry** against **cavalry** attacks.

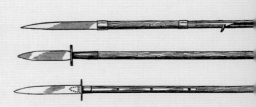

Firearms

Firearms were first invented in the 1400s. The first 'hand gonne' wasn't very useful and soldiers mostly preferred to use arrows and spears instead. It wasn't long before the musket was developed and, despite being quite difficult to load and fire, it became a very popular weapon.

Cannons

A cannon is a large tube-like gun that fires cannonballs – or anything that will fit into its tube – over great distances. By the 16th century, archery duels were slowly being replaced by **artillery exchanges** using cannons. Although archers were capable of doing great damage, it's easy to imagine how much more frightening a cannon duel was.

The battle of Shrewsbury

Date: 21 July 1403
Where: Shrewsbury, Shropshire
Why: revenge and power
Armies: House of Lancaster vs. a rebel army led by the Percy family
Who won: Lancastrians

C an you imagine you and your friends doing battle against one another, stopping at nothing to get what you want? It might seem unthinkable but when honour is at stake, anything can happen!

A sunny slaughter

600 years ago, in a field at Shrewsbury, the king of England and his once good friends, the powerful Percy family, did just that. And, as the sun set on that sunny summer evening, thousands of men lay dead in one of the biggest slaughters in English history: the battle of Shrewsbury.

Henry IV was often called Henry Bolingbroke or the Duke of Lancaster. This statue of him sits on Battlefield Church in Shrewsbury, as a reminder of the battle.

Just good friends?

The Percys had been good friends to Henry IV (**WW**) in the past. They had, after all, helped him to knock Richard II off the English throne. Now that's what friends are for! Henry rewarded the Percys, but not enough to their liking and this made them very angry. They thought that they were the 'uncrowned kings of the north-east' and deserved more land and power. Soon Henry and his good friends became deadly enemies.

Camp life at a medieval battle site wasn't much of a picnic!

Start of war

The Percy family decided that enough was enough: they wanted revenge for the way that Henry had treated them. So, they sent word to a Welsh **rebel** called Owen Glendower and asked him to help them fight the king. Owen agreed and it wasn't long before the Percys headed to meet him with an army of over 5,000 men, stopping on their way at Shrewsbury. Henry got wind of their plans whilst on his way to another battle but took a hasty detour to meet them.

Give peace a chance

The king came face-to-face with the Percys and tried to negotiate peace. He generously offered Harry Hotspur (**WW**), the leader of the family, 'peace and pardon'. Hotspur thought about the offer. He sent his uncle, Thomas Percy, with a list of demands for the king to which Henry agreed readily. Thomas, however, was still very bitter over the lack of payment for helping Henry in the past and wanted a fight, so he did a very sneaky thing: when he returned to Hotspur and the rest of his family, he told them that King Henry had said no to their demands. The Percys were furious and so the battle began!

Three of the main knights fighting in the battle were called Henry! Hotspur was one of them.

Arrow power

A violent archery duel started the bloodshed, killing many men. Both armies had hundreds upon hundreds of archers using their deadly longbows. Imagine the sky filled with thousands of arrows – the noise of them flying past your head must have been absolutely terrifying.

Skilled archers lined up ready for the sign to let loose their arrows.

Hotspur's chance?

When the arrows ran out, the two armies fell upon each other in a vicious hand-to-hand struggle. The noise, fear and confusion with so many men fighting would have been overwhelming. While the footmen of both armies desperately slashed and stabbed at their enemies, Hotspur tried to kill the king, but failed.

Suits of armour weighed about 25 kg. They may look difficult to move in but in fact, they were very flexible.

An account from the time of battle said that the sky was so full of arrows that they looked like a thick cloud blotting out the sun!

The English longbow

For many years English soldiers had used their mighty longbows to fight off their enemies with ease. Shrewsbury was the first battle, though, that saw English bowmen face each other with these mighty weapons.

Knights

A knight was a very important soldier. During the Middle Ages, noblemen were trained from a young age in the skills of knighthood. This meant that they spent hours learning how to handle weapons, **joust** and live according to a strict code of **chivalry**. When preparing for battle, it could take up to an hour to get dressed in full armour. If he was a loyal and successful knight, the rewards were great: a lady to marry, land, a castle and lots of money.

Boy soldier

King Henry's 15-year-old son, Henry, Prince of
Wales, was fighting with his father at Shrewsbury.
Through clever battle tactics they managed to
sandwich the rebels between them and it was this that
hastened the end of the battle. Then disaster struck –
the prince was hit by an arrow in the face! Bravely, he
carried on fighting, a sign that impressed his men, some
of whom had many years of fighting experience – a lot
more than young Henry. So they made one last
almighty attack on Hotspur's
rebel army – a move that
helped to win the battle.

🛡 It wasn't uncommon for
young boys like Henry to go into
battle. Henry was said to have
showed 'courage beyond his
years' at Shrewsbury.

Hotspur is dead!

Suddenly, a cry was heard that Harry Hotspur had been killed – by an

arrow. Some of the wiser Percy warriors knew
that all was lost and so they fled. Others had
no idea that the battle was over and carried
on fighting well into the night. The cry of
"No quarter!" (*see* page 37) went up and the
king's men started killing the fleeing rebels.

🛡 Stone soldiers on Shrewsbury
Church commemorate the men
who died in the battle.

The end has come!

The efforts of the last
rebel soldiers were in
vain. The king's men
were too powerful for
them. It had only
taken between two
and three hours for
the resistance to fall
apart, and for the
Percys to have well
and truly lost.

Is he dead yet?

King Henry displayed
Hotspur's dead body in
Shrewsbury town to let
everyone know about his victory.
He then cut off the head, arms and legs
and sent them to the four corners of the
country! It was months until the pieces
were finally returned for a proper burial,
which can't have been very pleasant. The
smell of rotting flesh and the sight of
hundreds of slimy maggots must
have been disgusting!

Battle tactics

t doesn't necessarily matter how many men you have or how good your weapons are, it's the tactics that you and your army use that can often make or break a battle.

BATTLE FACTS

Tactics are the clever thinking behind fighting. If William the Conqueror had sent his troops up Senlac Hill without good tactical orders they would have had no chance against Harold's shieldwall at the battle of Hastings. Good tactics separate brilliant leaders from rotten ones.

High ground

Position your army on high ground, such as on the top of a hill. This will almost always give you an advantage over your enemy and, if you occupy a very strong position, your enemy might even refuse to fight altogether. As well as giving you a good view, a slope gives extra oomph to your charges and slows down attacks from the enemy.

Reserves

Make sure that you have more men waiting to join the battle when you need them, like having a reserve on the bench in football. You can hide them, get them to wait at the back of the fight for their turn or get them to arrive later on.

Surprise attack

It's pretty hard work trying to march thousands of men with all their jingly-jangly armour and weapons – not to mention squeaky cannon wheels – towards the enemy for a surprise assault. What's more, in order to avoid being spotted by look-outs, you might have to do it in the dead of night. Getting the recipe right for a surprise attack is hard, so think carefully before you charge in.

Rumours

We all know that rumours can cause trouble. In battles they sometimes had disastrous consequences. Start a rumour and you could influence the fight in your favour, especially if you shout that the enemy leader is dead! The enemy soldiers could lose heart, flee and win you the battle.

Formation

Just like with a football team, an army needs to have a pattern of attack. Plan your formations well and you can surround your enemy more easily.

Great leaders

Finally, being a good leader isn't enough – you have to be a great one. You need to have the respect of your men and show them your own courage. Robert the Bruce, left, was one such great leader, who, with the support of his men, against huge odds, used skill and courage to obtain Scotland's independence from England.

The Wars of the Roses

The long, ugly and very bloody Wars of the Roses were a string of battles fought between the **House of Lancaster** and the **House of York,** who struggled with each other for the right to the English crown.

Why this war started

When Edward III (**WW**) died in 1377, his grandson Richard, Duke of York took over as Richard II. He reigned until another of Edward's grandsons – Lancastrian Henry Bolingbroke – stole the throne and became Henry IV.

🛡 Henry was the only child and heir of King Henry V.

Keep it in the family

The English throne stayed with the House of Lancaster until Henry VI (**WW**), who became king at the age of nine months old. It's very hard to rule a country when you're a baby, so others tried to claim the throne and England sank into corruption.

A poor king

When Henry VI *was* finally old enough to be a proper king, he was a weak one. He was surrounded by bad advisors and suffered from fits of madness. His wife, a French princess called Margaret of Anjou (**WW**), was thought to be the real power behind the throne at the time.

🛡 Useless Henry VI lost nearly all of England's land in France.

1455	1455–60	1461–70	1471–80	1481–87	1487
Wars of the Roses begin	1st St. Albans Blore Heath Ludford Bridge Northampton Wakefield	Mortimer's Cross 2nd St. Albans Ferrybridge Towton Hedgeley Moor Hexham Edgecote Moor Losecote Field	Barnet Tewkesbury	Bosworth	Stoke Wars of the Roses end

🛡 Wars of the Roses timeline showing the battles that happened. The battles in green are featured in this book.

Yorkists move in

Eventually, England had had enough of their rubbish Lancastrian king and the Yorkists thought that they should rule again. The first thing they did was to take advantage of King Henry's mad fits and make Richard Plantagnet, Duke of York, Lord Protector of England. This, of course, meant trouble and it wasn't long before the two families came to blows in battle.

Both Richard's parents were direct descendants of Edward III so he had a good claim to the throne.

Armies come to blows during a re-enactment of the Wars of the Roses.

Two kings spoil the broth

Despite being victorious three times in battle under the leadership of Richard, the House of York still hadn't got the throne. When Richard was killed in battle, all looked lost for them. Luckily people were fed up with Henry VI and so they welcomed Richard's son, Edward IV (**WW**) as king. Two kings for England? This was never going to work!

Years of war

England found itself in the middle of the Wars of the Roses and it was 27 years until the blood of the houses of Lancaster and York finally stopped flowing and England was at peace again.

The two roses

It's a myth that the name of the war comes from the pictures on the standards of the two rivals: a white rose for the Yorkists and a red one for the Lancastrians. In fact, the standards depicted a large variety of different symbols and icons – bulls, bears, boars, horses, greyhounds, dragons, lions and rams.

The battle of Towton

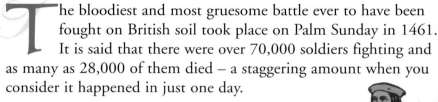

Date: 29 March 1461
Where: Towton, Yorkshire
Why: the right to the English throne
Armies: House of York vs. House of Lancaster
Who won: Yorkists

The bloodiest and most gruesome battle ever to have been fought on British soil took place on Palm Sunday in 1461. It is said that there were over 70,000 soldiers fighting and as many as 28,000 of them died – a staggering amount when you consider it happened in just one day.

Two kings go to war

Henry and Edward were both crowned king of England at the time. Towton was the chance to see who should be the one, true monarch. Henry was weak, so his queen, Margaret of Anjou, took charge of things for the House of Lancaster. She instructed the Duke of Somerset, Henry Beaufort (**WW**), to be her chief commander. For the House of York, Edward IV was in command. He, too, had support from two important nobleman – the Earl of Warwick, Richard Neville (**WW**), and the Duke of Norfolk, John Mowbray (**WW**).

Edward IV, like his father, was a great leader.

A Yorkist lord called Fauconberg orders his men to attack the Lancastrians with all their might.

Bad weather

It wasn't a good day for a battle – it was bitterly cold and a blizzard was raging. The weather would have caused lots of problems for the soldiers. Their hands would have been too cold to grip their weapons properly, for example. Also, the ice and the sludge would have made the ground very slippery and the blizzard would have made it difficult to see and judge distances.

Arrow attack

It took over four hours to get all the men ready. Even then, the Yorkist army was short of thousands of men, as Norfolk's troops were late. They launched their first attack anyway. Like a shot, Somerset's archers soon got organised. They let loose streams and streams of arrows until they had none left. Sadly for them, though, the strong, icy wind made the arrows fall short: the Lancastrians had lost the archery duel!

It is estimated that Fauconberg's archers would have sent over 100,000 arrows per minute into the enemy ranks.

The Lancastrians push back the Yorkist army.

The infantry attack

Seeing that the archers' assault had failed, Henry knew that he had to get his men engaged in actual fighting with Edward's. He gave the order and his infantry quickly launched a furious hand-to-hand attack, hacking their way ferociously through the Yorkist frontline.

Edward was tough on his enemies, unlike peace-loving Henry who thought that the battle ought to be postponed as it was Palm Sunday. Edward ordered the cry of

"No quarter!"

This meant that no mercy was to be given to the other side and even injured or surrendering soldiers were to be killed.

This re-enactment doesn't show the weather at the time of Towton, but can you imagine how difficult it must have been fighting in a blizzard?

Guts galore

By now the soldiers were fighting on a sea of bodies, sliding around on blood, guts and sludgy snow. Despite this, the Lancastrian army managed to break through the Yorkist left **flank**. At last they had strengthened their position in the fight.

More troops arrive

The bitter struggle carried on, the death toll grew by the minute and Henry's victory looked secure. Or did it? Luckily for Edward, and unknown to the Lancastrians, the Duke of Norfolk's troops had arrived at last and were ready to fight for the House of York.

Norfolk's troop arrive at last.

Legend has it that so many Lancastrians died in the river that other fleeing Lancastrians used their bodies as a bridge... and the river turned red with blood.

A river of blood

This was the turning point in the battle. Henry's men were dog-tired and began to flee. Many of them tried to escape by crossing the nearby river and, in the panic of doing so, were crushed by other soldiers or drowned by the icy waters.

Victory!

By nightfall, the battle was won by King Edward IV, leaving the heralds to count the thousands upon thousands of dead soldiers. The battlefield was so awash with blood and gore that, to this day, it is called 'Bloody Meadow'. Local legend says that when it snows on this land, the ghostly cries and moans of the dying soldiers can still be heard. That's spooky!

A knight stands ready for action even after the victory is called. You can never be too careful – the enemy might launch one last desperate attack.

Lucky or skilled?

Battle tactics were very important for the Yorkists' victory. They had the high ground, meaning that the Lancastrians had to fight uphill. From this position Edward and his men had the weather in their favour, with the wind driving the snow straight into the Lancastrians' eyes. They also had reinforcements, so that when the initial fighting men were tired, there were 'fresh legs' ready to take over. Despite this being unplanned, it was a lucky break that eventually helped to win the battle.

A Yorkist knight shouts a cry of victory.

Henry escapes

As for Henry VI and Queen Margaret, they fled to Scotland after the battle and then, when the dust had settled, they went abroad. Queen Margaret managed to get back to England to fight another day (*see* pages 44–47) but Henry was later captured by King Edward who banished him to the Tower of London, left, and to his death: Henry was murdered there and never breathed free air again.

The battle of Barnet

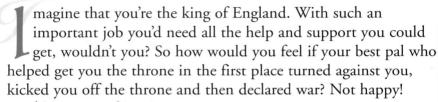

Date: 14 April 1471
Where: Barnet, Hertfordshire
Why: the right to the English throne
Armies: House of York vs. Warwick the Kingmaker
Who won: Yorkists

Imagine that you're the king of England. With such an important job you'd need all the help and support you could get, wouldn't you? So how would you feel if your best pal who helped get you the throne in the first place turned against you, kicked you off the throne and then declared war? Not happy!

🛡 Warwick owned lots of land, which gave him wealth and power.

Friends become enemies

King Edward IV had just that problem with his old friend Richard Neville – the powerful Earl of Warwick. Warwick had wanted Edward to marry a relative of the French king, Louis XI, to strengthen their ties with France. Edward secretly married a lady called Elizabeth Woodville, though. This made Warwick so angry that he drove Edward out of England – to France – and put Henry VI back on the throne.

Ed's back!

By the spring of 1471, however, Edward was back in England and ready to fight for the Yorkists again. With an army of nearly 10,000 men, he managed to regain control of London and it wasn't long before he and Warwick challenged each other to a day of reckoning – the battle of Barnet.

🛡 This map shows how the armies were positioned at the start of the battle and the noblemen who were in charge of each section of men.

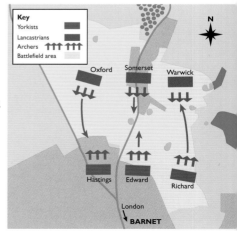

Key
Yorkists
Lancastrians
Archers ↟↟↟ ↟↟↟
Battlefield area

Oxford   Somerset   Warwick

Hastings   Edward   Richard

London
BARNET

N

Getting ready

Edward's Yorkist army arrived at Barnet the
night before the battle. Warwick and his
Lancastrian soldiers were already in position
with an 8,000-strong army, hidden from
Edward behind a ridge just north of the town.

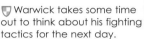 Warwick takes some time
out to think about his fighting
tactics for the next day.

Standards

A standard was a type of
battle flag that was popular
during **medieval** times. Each
one had some of the coat of
arms of the king or main
commanders on it and was
carried for the whole fight
by a standard bearer. A
bearer guarded the flag with
his life – if he dropped it,
others might think that this
signalled a defeat or that the
king was dead.

Too close for comfort

Unaware of this fact,
Edward set up his camp
much closer to Warwick
than he realised. During
the night, Warwick gave
the order to fire the
cannons at Edward's
camp but he didn't
know how close
Edward was and the
cannonballs overshot.
Lucky for Edward!

A real pea-souper

Thick, menacing fog rolled
in across Barnet early the
next day making it difficult
to see, let alone fight. The
leaders would have really
struggled to see how their
armies were fairing across
the field.

Night draws in and the cannons
thunder as Warwick tries to get
an early shot at Edward.

Not a clue

Both armies' left flanks fell early in the battle but neither Warwick nor Edward knew a thing about that because of the bad fog. Victory was going to be tough, but what happened next

The Kingmaker

The Earl of Warwick was nicknamed 'the Kingmaker'. This was because he used his great wealth and power to help put both Edward IV and Henry VI on the English throne – depending on which side he wanted to be on at the time, of course!

certainly meant that victory for the Lancastrians was in total jeopardy...

Fighting in dense fog must have been terrifying for the men at Barnet.

Loot to boot

The Earl of Oxford, one of Warwick's main commanders, and his men had been hounding Yorkists who had fled to Barnet – and doing a spot of looting on the side! This was quite common in battles where one side fled and the other chased – often for miles on end.

Mistaken identity

On their return to the main battle, Oxford and his men were the victims of mistaken identity. The fog made it difficult to see who was who and the soldiers' identifying badges all looked the same. Oxford's own comrades thought that he and his men were Yorkists, not Lancastrians, and so they turned on each other, slashing, stabbing and firing at close quarters.

A wounded soldier is taken away to safety.

Traitors?

"Treason!" came the cry from the Lancastrians – they were flabbergasted at their own men trying to kill them. Disheartened, many ran from the battlefield. To make matters worse, both armies had fallen out of line and were positioned badly so it was difficult for the leaders to see what was going on or to call any order. Some of Warwick's men even thought that their comrades had actually swapped sides and were now fighting for Edward as traitors – what a mess!

Warwick loses

The damage done by this case of mistaken identity was massive. Up until that point in the battle, it looked as though Warwick might win. Now, that was never going to happen. With many of his men in disarray or dead, Warwick had lost the battle of Barnet.

🛡 Wearing the sign of your leader helped with identification in battle if the two sides didn't have uniforms. Sadly, the fog at Barnet meant that this didn't help the Lancastrians.

🛡 The Yorkists march home feeling exhausted but victorious.

Defeat!

At last the mists started to clear to reveal a bloody scene as over 1,500 men had been slain: 1,000 Lancastrians and 500 Yorkists. Warwick was dead, Oxford and his men had fled and the battle was over. Barnet only lasted about three or four hours but it was a terrible defeat for the Lancastrians and they lost their most powerful supporter – the Earl of Warwick.

The battle of Tewkesbury

Date: 4 May 1471
Where: Tewkesbury, Gloucestershire
Why: the right to the English throne
Armies: House of York vs. House of Lancaster
Who won: Yorkists

Only two weeks after Barnet, Edward IV had yet another battle on his hands. Queen Margaret of Anjou had arrived back from France with 17 ships full of men all ready to fight for her against King Edward to ensure that her young son, Edward, Prince of Wales, (WW) would be the next king of England.

Margaret's cause

Margaret, under the House of Lancaster, had to rely on the Duke of Somerset to lead her army. He was the only well-experienced knight fighting for Margaret and this meant problems. The king was a skilled soldier with many skilled knights – would Margaret be able to outwit or outfight him? Probably not...

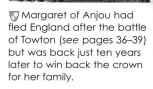

Margaret of Anjou had fled England after the battle of Towton (see pages 36–39) but was back just ten years later to win back the crown for her family.

Clever Ed

Edward's men were exhausted from marching to Tewkesbury *and* they were outnumbered – they had about 2,000 less men than the Lancastrians. Edward needed a good tactic to get the upper hand. He decided to hide 200 of his cavalry behind some trees – these reinforcements would be very useful later on in the fight.

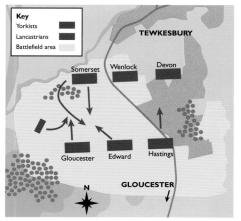

Key
Yorkists
Lancastrians
Battlefield area

TEWKESBURY

Somerset   Wenlock   Devon

Gloucester   Edward   Hastings

GLOUCESTER

N

This map shows the movement of the two armies and the commanding noble

The strings of a longbow were usually made from flax, hemp or silk.

Edward attacks

The battle started with a ferocious attack by Edward's men from the air – first with deadly arrows and then with an onslaught of cannon balls. Edward's army had much better artillery than their enemy – an advantage that helped them get off to a good start.

Somerset loses his rag

Somerset **counter-attacked** using the hills and ditches of the battlefield as a cover but he soon began to struggle. He'd been relying on his ally Lord Wenlock who was actually leading the Lancastrian centre to back him up – but Wenlock didn't appear! Had he backed out from his deal at the last minute? Historians aren't sure but Somerset thought he had and was furious.

Somerset's men get pushed back fiercely by Edward's infantry.

Tewkesbury axe

This axe was found at the site of the battle of Tewkesbury by a farmer with his metal detector. It is a battle axe, dates from around 1375–1450 and is made of iron.

Historians believe that it could have been used at the battle.

Hidden force

It was now that Edward's hidden soldiers showed their faces. They galloped out from their wooded hiding place and attacked Somerset from behind. It was all too much and Somerset's men began to run away.

Lord 'Wavering' Wenlock

Lord Wenlock had been a ditherer for some time. He had first fought on the Yorkist side at Towton and then on the Lancastrian side here at Tewkesbury. When he failed to help Somerset in his charge, the angry Duke thought that Wenlock might have changed sides again. He threatened to hit Wenlock on the head with his axe and dash out his brains!

Did Somerset get hold of Wenlock and carry out his threat?

Sound the horns!

Edward regrouped and set about getting rid of the rest of the Lancastrians. He ordered trumpets to be sounded and his men lunged forward in search of their enemy. They were so determined and so frightening that it wasn't long before the rest of Margaret's army joined in the desperate struggle to escape.

The trumpets blasted and the men attacked.

A difficult escape

The soldiers that fled had many obstacles to overcome – uneven ground, the town, the nearby abbey and the River Severn all stood in the way of a quick escape. A huge number of men were killed at Tewkesbury, leaving the battlefield in such a terrible mess, that it, like Towton, was known ever after as 'Bloody Meadow'.

The soldiers lunge at each other in close combat.

The Yorkist army are jubilant. It had been a tough fight, but they had had better skilled men and more efficient weapons.

No quarter!

The Yorkists sensed that victory was theirs and cried "No quarter!". Historical accounts state that possibly as many as 2,000 Lancastrian soldiers may have died that day. The Yorkist army came off much better – their losses probably totalled no more than 500.

Prisoners

The Lancastrians lost almost all of their important people in the slaughter that followed the battle. The Duke of Somerset was dragged out of hiding and killed; Edward, Prince of Wales, was also murdered and his mother, Queen Margaret, was captured. Henry VI, imprisoned in the Tower of London at the time, was murdered too.

Survivors line up after the battle ready to go home.

All is lost

The Lancastrian cause was lost after the battle of Tewkesbury and England was at peace for a while. It would be another 14 years before the two houses of Lancaster and York would fight again over the right to the English crown.

Edward rules!

The only surviving Lancastrian claimants to the throne were Jasper Tudor (WW) and his nephew Henry Tudor (WW). They both had fled to France, though, and were no threat to Edward IV. He ruled until his death in 1483, never having to fight for his crown again.

The battle of Bosworth

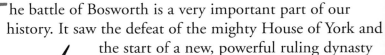

Date: 22 August 1485
Where: Bosworth, Leicestershire – but actual site unknown
Why: the right to the English throne
Armies: House of York vs. House of Lancaster
Who won: Lancastrians

The battle of Bosworth is a very important part of our history. It saw the defeat of the mighty House of York and the start of a new, powerful ruling dynasty – the **Tudors**, with Henry Tudor as king.

The young prince

In 1483 12-year-old Edward V took over the English throne – a pretty important job for a young boy! Edward's reign didn't last long however, as his conniving uncle Richard pinched the crown and became Richard III.

🛡 Despite his young age, Edward was determined to be a good leader.

Henry returns

The news of Richard's treachery soon reached the ears of Henry Tudor who was still living in France. Henry decided to invade England on behalf of the House of Lancaster, starting the Wars of the Roses again.

🛡 The Yorkist flag flies proudly above the soldiers.

The princes in the tower

Edward IV's oldest son was only king for a couple of months. After his uncle had taken the throne from him, Richard imprisoned Edward and his younger brother in the Tower of London. No one is really sure what happened to them after this – were they murdered? Two small skeletons found in the Tower years later suggest this may be true – and if so, by whom? Their story, often referred to as 'the princes in the tower' is one of history's favourite mysteries.

A shaky start

The two warring armies met on a sweltering hot day at a town called Market Bosworth. The start of the battle was difficult for the king. He wasn't a popular leader and his army didn't seem to be totally on his side. Indeed, at one point during the fight, a strong ally of his – Lord Stanley (**WW**) – let him down by not attacking the enemy when he was supposed to.

The infantry of the two armies come face-to-face.

Attack!

The Duke of Norfolk was in charge of some of Richard's men. He lead a mighty charge down the hill into Henry's general, the Earl of Oxford. Oxford didn't have as many men as Norfolk did, so he quickly closed in the lines of his men to have any chance of a good defence.

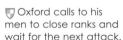

Oxford calls to his men to close ranks and wait for the next attack.

Henry is spotted

Through the gap that this left, however, King Richard spied Henry Tudor and decided to attack him! Richard charged directly at Henry, almost reaching him, but the force of the battle swept him away and prevented his assault.

The dead are left for now, as the battle is still in progress. They will be buried later.

The king's defeat

The reason that Lord Stanley hadn't attacked before was because he hadn't yet decided who he really wanted to fight for! He soon made up his mind, though, and joined Henry. His decision sealed the king's fate: Stanley's 3,000-strong force crashed into Richard's once formidable army. The Yorkist army fell apart and fled.

Richard's last stand

The king refused to run and stayed on his horse. Then tragedy struck: his horse got trapped in the bloody, boggy marsh and, even though he fought bravely, the king was doomed. Rebel soldiers quickly finished him off and grabbed the crown for Henry.

Richard tries to keep fighting. Little does he know that he is about to be killed.

Trimming

What Lord Stanley did was known as 'trimming'. This meant sitting on the fence until you could be sure which side was going to win, and then jumping on the victorious bandwagon! Even so, his decision was hugely important to the outcome of the battle. His 3,000 men had the power to totally swing the result, and both Richard and Henry were very anxious to get him on side. It's very surprising he even thought about it, though, as Henry was actually his son-in-law.

Stanley finds Richard's crown and holds it aloft for the new king of England.

Let's party!

So, Richard was dead, his army had all but run away and Henry's men were the victors. With the crown on his head, the new king addressed his tired but triumphant troops. It must have been some party that night to celebrate their victory.

🛡 Combatant signs at Bosworth battlesite show the coats of arms of the major commanders involved in the battle.

The Tudor reign

The long and bloody Wars of the Roses had all but come to an end. Henry and his Tudor family, which included many famous future kings and queens – such as Henry VIII (WW) and Elizabeth I – stayed in power for a full 18 years.

🛡 King Richard's well – Richard was supposed to have drank from the spring under this well during the battle.

Medieval munching

Medieval food was very different from the food of today: no pizzas, no hamburgers and you were expected to eat with your hands! Beef and mutton were very popular and there would have been plenty of fruit and veg. Instead of plates, pieces of hard bread were often used that would soak up the blood and gravy from the meat. Yummy!

Music in battle

Imagine trying to tell a friend something when he's half a mile away from you with no mobile phone to help. You can't even use Morse code, because it hasn't been invented yet. That's exactly what it was like hundreds of years ago when a battle commander wanted to give orders to his men.

Chinese whispers

Shouting commands sometimes worked but when your army was stretched out over two miles with the wind carrying away your voice and men screaming war cries, it was very hard to be heard. You could pass a message through the ranks but that could lead to 'Chinese whispers' and your message would end up very different to how it had started. The answer lay in music: leaders recruited musicians to play certain types of music to mean different orders and also to give the soldiers courage.

Trumpets

A 'tuquet' was a trumpet call that was used to signal the cavalrymen to charge.

Drums

The drum and the type of beat used on it also helped to tell the cavalrymen that they needed to attack.

Bagpipes

The Celtic bagpipe was a sacred instrument in Scotland and Scottish armies never marched without one. It was considered almost a weapon in itself. In fact, after Culloden, the English courts ruled it as such and bagpipe-playing was against the law!

Giving courage

Music wasn't just for giving orders, it was a great giver of courage. When faced with the dreadful, brutal task ahead of them, it lifted the soldier's spirits and gave them a valuable sense of **camaraderie**. They had often been marching for days to get to a battlefield and had few home comforts once there. Music was a great help.

Roman music

The cornu was a type of horn used for battle and ceremonial purposes that was introduced into Britain by the Romans. It was made from a long, brass tube which was twisted into the shape of a 'G'.

No news

With no television or newspapers to tell people the details of a battle, poems and songs were written in memory of the event, like the Maldon poem (*see* page 17). They told what had happened, who had won and, perhaps most importantly, the tragedy of the lives lost.

The English Civil War

The English **Civil War** started in 1642 and started as a result of a long-running argument between King Charles I (WW) and **Parliament** about how to run the country.

The republic

The king believed that he could do whatever he wanted. Parliament, on the other hand, didn't agree. They wanted Charles to rule in a fair and traditional way. Charles sort of tried to follow their wishes but it wasn't long before he proved himself to be untrustworthy again. Little did he know that if he didn't buck up his ideas, he could face execution…

Charles in charge

Charles, however, wanted things his own way and started to make some unpopular decisions. When Parliament tried to put their foot down, the king stopped asking them for advice and **dissolved** them. With the nosey Parliament out of the way Charles almost had ultimate power and answered to no one but himself.

Charles I was the son of James I and Anne of Denmark. He became king of England at the age of 25.

Charles weds

Charles loved being king. He spent lots of money and expected the people of England to pay for his lavish lifestyle. He married an interfering and influential French princess – Henrietta Maria – against the advice of his peers and friends. Henrietta Maria, like Charles, was very strong-willed and before long, the royal couple were starting to cause real problems.

Queen Henrietta Maria of France.

War!

On one occasion, Henrietta Maria told Charles to arrest five members of Parliament. This was a stupid move and support for Parliament grew stronger because of it. Eventually, Charles was forced to leave London and gather together an army to defend his right to be king. This was the start of the long and bloody English Civil War.

🛡 Amongst others, Charles tried to imprison the important politician John Hampden.

Believers

Those people who believed in and would fight for the Church of England and the king were called Cavaliers. Those who thought that Parliament were right and were willing to die for their cause were called Roundheads.

🛡 Tension between the king and Parliament leads to war.

Civil War

The war happened in three parts:

🛡 **1642–1646 – the Great Civil War:** this was the main war between Charles I and Parliament's army. Charles lost.

🛡 **1648 – the Second Civil War:** Charles refused to reach a peaceful agreement with Parliament. This led to another Civil War. Charles lost this battle as well – and his head – and England became a republic under Oliver Cromwell (**WW**).

🛡 **1650–1651 – the Third Civil War:** Charles' son, Charles II (**WW**), took up his father's fight and challenged Parliament again. He lost against Cromwell.

1642–1643	1644–1645	1648–1649	1650–1651
Civil War begins	Marston Moor	St. Fagans	Worcester
Edgehill	2nd Newbury	Preston	Civil War ends
Chalgrove Field	Naseby		
Adwalton Moor			
Roundway Down			
1st Newbury			

🛡 The Civil War timeline showing the battles that happened during the English Civil War.

The battle of Edgehill

Date: 23 October 1642
Where: Edgehill, Warwickshire
Why: control of the government of England
Armies: Royalist army vs. Parliamentarian army
Who won: Royalists

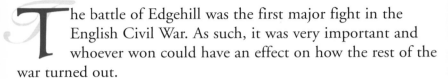

The battle of Edgehill was the first major fight in the English Civil War. As such, it was very important and whoever won could have an effect on how the rest of the war turned out.

The armies meet
The Parliamentarian army of the Earl of Essex came to blows with the Royalist army of King Charles, led by the feared and courageous Prince Rupert (WW) not far from the village of Kineton.

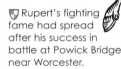

🛡 The Earl of Essex, Robert Devereux.

🛡 Young soldiers line up ready to fight. Imagine going to war at such a young age.

🛡 Rupert's fighting fame had spread after his success in battle at Powick Bridge near Worcester.

Forming for battle
The two armies were equally matched – each with about 13–14,000 men. They both arranged their troops in the same way: infantry in the centre, cavalry and **dragoons** on the flanks. The battle started on a steep hill called Edgehill. The Royalists started out on the top of the hill and the Earl of Essex spread out his men at Kineton.

Let loose the cannons!

Essex didn't move an inch. He watched and he waited. And waited and waited... Finally, the curious Royalists started to come down the hill to

meet him. Essex didn't lose a second of this advantage and gave the command to let loose the artillery. The Parliamentarian's booming cannons blasted away for about an hour, letting rip their deadly accurate cannonballs.

An experienced soldier could load and fire his gun four times a minute. That was fast!

Advance!

As the mists of the artillery fire started to clear, the king's dragoons began to advance, closely followed by his fearsome cavalry. Then disaster struck: some of the Parliamentarian cavalry joined the Royalist side. Essex must have been livid!

Is this the end?

Suddenly, it seemed as if some of Essex's men were giving up. His infantry started to flee the battlefield. Was the mighty Parliamentarian army defeated?

Musketeer

A musketeer, or musketman, used a gun called a musket as his weapon during battle. He would hold it against his shoulder to fire it, using small lead balls with gunpowder inside them for bullets. Musketeers practised hard at their battle tactics. They learnt how to automatically follow orders and move accurately and quickly in tight formation.

🛡 Prince Rupert desperately tries to rally his men – this is no time to run away.

Shop 'til you drop

Lucky for Essex, the answer was no. The king's cavalry were keen that no one got away and chased after the fleeing Parliamentarians without a second thought. Rupert must have only been able to watch in dismay as they left him and the rest of his men unprotected. It is probable that his men charged all the way into Kineton village and looted supplies there rather than returning to the battle. This was not the time for shopping, though!

Attack!

Without the cavalry, the remaining Royalists were weak and open to vicious attacks from both the front and back. Now it was the turn of the Royalists to lose heart.

🛡 A 17th-century silver coin found during a dig at Edgehill. It is possibly connected with the battle.

🛡 Being stuck in the middle of hand-to-hand combat was noisy and frightening.

Cannon fodder

What had looked like certain victory for Rupert and the king was now a bit more difficult to call, and Essex's artillery men weren't beaten yet. They stuffed whatever they could find into their cannons and fired at Rupert's men.

Essex at the front

Once the two armies' infantry clashed, the commanders of each army had almost no control over the action – it became a desperate heave-ho, with each side frantically slashing and hacking at the enemy to try and save their own lives. Normally the officers took a back seat at this stage, but at Edgehill the Earl of Essex fought with his men on the frontline.

⬦ A GPS machine used to find the position of finds at Edgehill.

⬦ Essex bravely joins the frontline and fights in the thick of the action.

The battle result

Despite the king's losses, he still had a formidable army. Essex felt beaten and decided to pull back and save what men he had left. The Royalist cavalry got back just in time from their looting in Kineton to witness their victory, but there were no celebrations. Both sides knew the king had scraped through by the skin of his teeth and that there would probably be many more battles to come.

Cavaliers and Roundheads

We use the terms Parliamentarians and Royalists in this book but the nicknames for each army during the English Civil War were the Roundheads (Parliamentarians) and Cavaliers (Royalists). It is thought that the Roundheads, like this soldier right, were named because of their short hair, and the Cavaliers, left, from a Spanish word for being 'no good'.

Historians also now believe that the two sides probably wore very similar uniforms.

The battle of Marston Moor

Date: 2 July 1644
Where: Marston Moor, Yorkshire
Why: control of the government of England
Armies: Royalist army vs. Parliamentarian army
Who won: the Parliamentarians

T wo years after the battle of Edgehill the Civil War was in full swing for control over northern England. The Parliamentarian army led by Sir Thomas Fairfax (**WW**) had **besieged** York – one of the most important cities in the country.

🚩 Fairfax was general of the Parliamentarian forces in the north of England

Rupert to the rescue

It was a desperate situation so they sent an urgent request to London for back-up. None other than Prince Rupert came to the rescue on behalf of the king. Despite being outnumbered, he craftily outwitted Thomas Fairfax and saved York from the clutches of Parliament.

🚩 Cromwell was a brave and respected commander who genuinely cared about the welfare of his men.

Let's fight

That wasn't the end of the fighting, however. Both leaders decided to challenge each other to battle again, this time at Marston Moor. Rupert arrived with about 14,000 men in tow and had another 4,000 more join him later in the day. Even with this vast number of men, he still had the smaller army, though. The Parliamentarians were a 28,000-strong force led by Alexander Leslie, the Earl of Leven. One of Leven's most important commanders was Oliver Cromwell.

Leven's men move into battle.

The battle begins

The two armies seemed unsure of how to start the battle and watched each other cautiously for most of the day. By the early evening, the Royalists were bored and, thinking that the battle was going to begin the next day, started to relax. That was the moment the Parliamentarians had been waiting for! They advanced at a startlingly quick pace down onto the moor to attack the Royalists.

Hooves of thunder

Hurriedly the Royalists gathered themselves together. Despite being unprepared for the attack, Prince Rupert's cavalry were ready in no time. They braced themselves as Oliver Cromwell's cavalry (known as the **Ironsides**) galloped towards them at a frightening speed, sending their horsemen into chaos and fear. Rupert tried to perk up his troops and ordered them to attack but 800 enemy cavalrymen blocked their path – an impenetrable power!

The Ironsides have done their damage and left carnage on the battlefield.

Hide and seek

In the bloody fighting and chaos that followed, Rupert's horse was cut down beneath him. Rupert ran for his life and spent the rest of the battle hiding in a bean field!

A young pikeman stands ready for battle. Pikemen often attacked in large square 'hedgehog' formations, tightly packed together for safety.

No back-up

Cromwell's horsemen were packed tightly together in what must have looked a very menacing force. Things were getting bleaker and bleaker for the Royalist army. On the other side of the field, however, they were doing slightly better, with their cavalry winning a charge. Then they started to chase after the enemy, though, leaving their foot soldiers without back-up.

The foot soldiers go in for the kill

The infantry brace themselves for the attack.

What a plan!

Despite this, the Royalists were winning the infantry battle, causing the Parliamentarians to think about giving up. Suddenly, Sir Thomas Fairfax had a cunning plan! He tore off his Parliamentarian sash so that no one knew who he was and slipped quietly through the enemy's front ranks to get to Cromwell.

Charge!

Fairfax finally found Cromwell behind the front and together they led a final, terrifying charge against the back of the Royalist infantry. It was a success. The Royalists were in a mess: all their remaining horses ran away and their foot soldiers were slashed to pieces.

Soldiers in formation use their weapons to maximum effect.

Whitecoats

At the time of Marston Moor, regiments' uniforms were paid for by the person who commanded them. Commanders often chose bright colours to distinguish their men. The Whitecoats, however, had undyed woollen cloth uniforms – so that's where they got their name from.

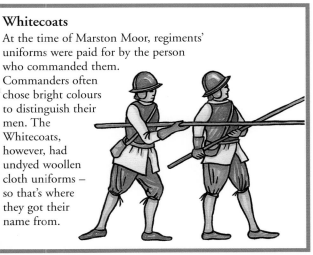

Standing firm

When this happened, one set of Royalist units valiantly stood their ground. These were the Whitecoats led by the Marquis of Newcastle. They held firm against furious attacks for over an hour until the Parliamentarians broke through their ranks and started to slaughter them. Not one Whitecoat fled the battlefield, however. It was only when their ammunition ran out that the remaining few men accepted their fate and were killed.

The king's terrible loss

The Parliamentarians hardly lost any men at Marston Moor, unlike the Royalists who lost over 4,000 with over another 1,000 being captured. These were staggering amounts. Raising an army of this size again would be tough for the king. With this win, the Parliamentarians gained vital control over the entire north of England. What a terrible defeat for Charles!

Many lie dead as the battle comes to an end.

The battle of Naseby

Date: 14 June 1645
Where: Naseby, Northamptonshire
Why: control of the government of England
Armies: Royalist army vs. Parliamentary army
Who won: the Parliamentarians

Following his great skill and bravery at Marston Moor, Sir Thomas Fairfax was made commander of a very special army – the New Model Army.

Naseby begins

King Charles I and Parliament were still at war with each other over how England should be governed. Fairfax had a tough job ahead of him helping to sort that out. With the massive fighting power of his new army, he got straight to work and planned a siege of Charles' headquarters in Oxford – a daring scheme!

A waxwork model of Charles I.

Standard bearers marching to battle.

Clever clogs

Fairfax's troops outnumbered the king's by two to one so the Parliamentarian leader was in a strong position. Charles was cunning, though, and tried to distract Fairfax from Oxford by storming the Parliamentarian **stronghold** of Leicester. His clever strategy worked – Fairfax quickly forgot about Oxford and a battle at Naseby was the result.

The New Model Army

The New Model Army was created in 1645 because the Parliamentarians thought that a professional army was the way to gain victories. At the time, there was a big difference between them and normal armies. Normal armies were recruited locally from wherever the battle was to be fought. The New Model Army, however, was a national army that was stationed in one place and then moved around as they were needed. Quite often, prisoners from other armies were forced to join the New Model Army and fight for their enemy.

Scouting

The land between the enemy armies was very hilly and neither side could see each other very well. Prince Rupert set off on a scouting mission to find the Parliamentarians – and they did the same. On the way he bumped into a few Parliamentarian scouts, and, thinking that the enemy were retreating, decided that his army should attack the next morning.

🛡 Rupert rides off and try to find the enemy camp.

Ready for battle

As the sun rose, the Royalists bravely advanced. It must have been a frightening surprise when they reached the bottom of a hill to see Fairfax's enormous army spread out above them ready for battle!

🛡 Fairfax's men line up and await their enemy.

Rupert's charge

Prince Rupert launched a death-defying charge up the hill. He quickly smashed through the Parliamentarian's cavalry and sent them fleeing for their lives!

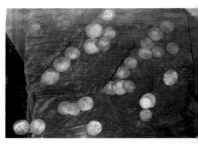
Prince Rupert charges towards the enemy at lightening speed.

Hot pursuit

Then, in true Royalist style, Rupert and his men left their foot soldiers to deal with the scary consequences of the charge, and set off in pursuit of the scattered enemy cavalry.

Royalists fight back

In the middle of the field it was a different story. Here, the Parliamentarian infantry were faced with blind courage and brute force from the Royalist infantry.

The musketeers of the New Model Army fire on the Royalist soldiers.

Reserves come in handy

Fairfax and his men tried desperately not to lose heart as they were pushed, step by step, back up the hill. Luckily, they were rescued by Henry Ireton (WW) and his cavalry who launched a fearsome charge, weakening the Royalist spirit. When Cromwell's reserves also charged forward, all seemed lost for the king and his men.

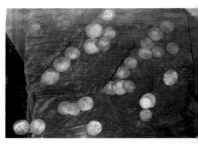
The Sibbertoft hoard – these coins were buried in the soil at Naseby for safe-keeping before the battle.

The death toll mounts but the fight is nearly over.

Run for your lives!

Some of the king's most loyal troops hung on but when they were also sliced down, the battle was well and truly at an end. Despite wanting to stay and face his enemy, the king's advisers convinced Charles to flee.

The losses

Charles' army lost around 1,000 of their 12,000 men, but for the Parliamentarians it had been a successful day. They lost just 150 men from their 15,000-strong force. The Parliamentarians had clinched another amazing victory but the war was still not quite won…

Shot from muskets found at the battlesite during a dig.

Uniforms

A Civil War soldier would have worn an iron back and breast plate, gauntlets and a thick leather buscoat. Mind you, he could count himself lucky if he had a full uniform – many wore their everyday clothes which offered little or no protection against spears or bullets.

The battle of Worcester

Date: 3 September 1651
Where: Worcester, Worcestershire
Why: control of the government of England
Armies: Royalist army vs. Parliamentarian army
Who won: the Parliamentarians

The last time that the Royalist and Parliamentarian armies ever met on the battlefield happened in the same place as their very first small skirmish in 1642: Worcestershire.

🚩 Some people think that Charles II was the greatest English monarch ever.

🚩 A statue of Cromwell in Westminster, London.

Help from the Scots

Charles II turned to Scotland for help this time in a fight against Cromwell. He, his main commander, Sir David Leslie, and 12,000 Scotsmen holed themselves up within the city walls of Worcester.

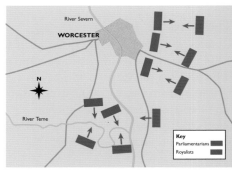
🚩 Battle map showing the positions and movement of troops.

Battle begins

The battle began at lots of different places at once, all on the outskirts of the city, before moving into the city streets. As the battle began, the king thought that he was in a strong position. He and Leslie had destroyed the bridges over the River Severn into the city and hoped that Cromwell's army would be forced to attack the strong eastern walls at Sidbury Gate where the king and his men would be waiting for them.

Hard luck, Charles

Charles was out of luck on that score, though. Cromwell was wise to his plan and wasn't going to let the river stand in the way of a good fight. So, he built temporary bridges so that his army could get into the city.

⛨ Soldiers march to Worcester.

Secret plan

This quick route into Worcester was useful for Cromwell. He was able to secretly send some of his men through the south-west part of the city without Charles knowing whilst he started the main battle in the east.

⛨ A soldier practicing with his weapon in preparation for battle.

Life in camp

Camps that were set up near the battlefields could be quite lavish. Tents for the king and main commanders in particular would have been well-guarded and contained some home comforts, such as thick bedding for cold nights and plenty of hearty food and drink.

🛡 Soldiers in formation with their pikes.

Cromwell's smart move

Cromwell's surprise assault didn't quite work, however. His men met fierce and unexpected opposition from the enemy and so Cromwell had to leave the main battle to help them. Despite this unwise decision to move from the main fighting area, Cromwell was on a roll. He helped his men in the south-west and then returned, beating back the king's men through Sidbury Gate – what a fast operator!

Run for your lives!

At the same time, more of Cromwell's men were advancing through the south side of the city. Their attacks were overpowering and the king's army there started to flee.

Throwing in the towel

The Royalist hopes were ruined! By now, Charles' men made little attempt to fight back – in fact, it was said by one witness that they were more likely to kill one another in their desperate search for escape rather than to have a go at their frightening enemy! Leslie looked like a broken man and refused to fight anymore, even though Charles pleaded with, and even threatened, him.

🛡 Boscobel Hou where Charles stayed when he fled the battle.

Charles scarpers

The city turned into a bloody hunt of the Royalists by the Parliamentarians. Charles II managed to make his escape to the safety of France. Back in Worcester, however, the victorious Oliver Cromwell and his New Model Army had won this last battle and the 11-year-long Civil War was finally at an end.

The dust starts to clear – the Parliamentarians have won the day.

It's a hard life

England became a very boring place under Cromwell's harsh rule. Unlike Charles, he disapproved of having fun and wanted the people of England to take life more seriously. He forced theatres and pubs to close and even banned maypole dancing! It's no surprise that when King Charles II was restored to the throne years later, people were ecstatic at the thought of some fun returning to their humdrum lives.

A dictator after all?

The English Civil War, and the fact that Parliament won it, had enormous consequences on England. The country had become a republic with Cromwell eventually ruling it as Lord Protector. This meant that he was king in all but name, though. Cromwell had absolute rule over Parliament, the Church and the English people, and he even wanted his son, Richard, to succeed him. In fact, he had become exactly the thing he had fought against in the war – an all-powerful dictator!

Part of the city wall at Worcester still stands today despite the battle damage.

Women in battle

BATTLE FACTS

Women have only recently been allowed into our modern-day British army, but back in Celtic times, legendary women warriors went to battle with the men. What's more, they fought naked!

Body search

It's true that men did most of the fighting in battles but women played their part, too. It was common for whole families to go to a battle and, when husbands didn't return from a fight, it was the wives' gruesome job to search through the blood, gore and dead bodies to find them.

Women warriors

Women didn't always stand on the sidelines though. Throughout history ordinary women to aristocratic ladies have helped protect their land and rights. In the 11th century, for example, Matilda of Ramsbury guarded Salisbury Castle and in the 1500s Lady Knyvet single-handedly defended her home of Buckingham Castle in Norfolk.

Women warriors

During the Wars of the Roses (*see* pages 34–51) it was feisty Queen Margaret, right, who was the real force behind the Lancastrian might – not King Henry. During the English Civil War women played even more important roles at the frontlines, such as gun reloading and carrying ammunition supplies.

Queen Henrietta Maria

Henrietta Maria was Charles I's feisty French queen. She had clear ideas on how England should be run and tried to help Charles make good political decisions. She also helped to raise money in Europe to fund the king's army and, despite sometimes getting in Charles' way and angering the English court, proved herself to be more than just a pretty face.

Boudicca

Another woman made famous by her skill at battle was the Iceni ruler Boudicca. Fed up with the suffering that the Romans were inflicting on her people, she launched a furious attack against them. The might of the Romans was too much, though, and Boudicca was defeated. In one last show of rebelliousness, she refused to let the Romans rejoice over their victory and took her own life!

The Jacobite Uprisings

It wasn't long before another civil war reared its ugly head. Even though Charles II's reign was a peaceful one, his death in 1685 made people think about who should be king next. As usual, this spelt war!

The 'Merry Monarch'

Charles II lived up to his nickname of the Merry Monarch. He had countless mistresses and many illegitimate children. This wasn't that unusual but the trouble was that he had no legitimate heirs to the throne. The only person who could lawfully succeed him was his brother, but he was Catholic.

Religion

The prospect of a Catholic king was cause for concern. He might

 Princess Diana of Wales was a descendant of Charles II, above.

try to restore the Catholic religion to England, which at the time was Protestant. This would be terrible for people who weren't Catholic as they would have to deny their religious beliefs.

Rumours

So, while Charles was still alive, Parliament spread rumours that he was married to the mother of his eldest son James Scott, the Duke of Monmouth (**WW**). This, of course, was totally untrue and even Charles denied the rumour – but it meant that Monmouth could be crowned king.

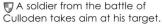 A soldier from the battle of Culloden takes aim at his target.

Monmouth

When Charles eventually died in 1685, however, his brother, James Stuart (WW), was crowned King James II – much to the anger of many people who thought that Monmouth should be on the throne. Parliament thought hard about what to do and eventually decided to persuade the Duke of Monmouth to challenge King James in battle (*see* pages 76–79).

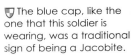 Mary (II) and William are crowned king and queen of England, Ireland and Scotland. Mary was the eldest daughter of Charles I and Henrietta Maria (see pages 54–55).

James is sacked!

Monmouth never became king, though, and after just three years of rule by James II, Parliament **overthrew** him and gave the crown to his daughter, Mary, and her Dutch husband, William of Orange.

The Stuarts' anger

This made the Stuarts furious. Along with many supporters, they spent the next 60 years trying to get the throne back for their family. They had settled in Europe at the time and used their allies in France and Spain to help them.

The uprisings

The Stuarts' and their supporters' attempts to get back the English throne happened in a series of revolts that came to be known as the Jacobite Uprisings.

 The blue cap, like the one that this soldier is wearing, was a traditional sign of being a Jacobite.

The battle of Sedgemoor

Date: 6 July 1685
Where: Westonzoyland, Somerset
Why: to remove a Catholic sovereign from the throne
Armies: Royalist army vs. Jacobite rebel army
Who won: Royalists

I n July 1685 there was more trouble with the English throne. King James II had enemies – enemies powerful enough and determined enough to take the crown from him and give it to James Scott, Duke of Monmouth.
This, of course, was treason!

Monmouth arrives

The king's enemies persuaded Monmouth that this plot was in England's best interests. Monmouth wasn't really interested in what they wanted, but thought he should try to help. He left his home in Holland and headed by ship to the west coast of England.

🛡 A plot in 1683 to kill James Stuart by his Protestant enemies was foiled and actually helped to make people more sympathetic to him becoming king.

The king's army

Monmouth landed in Lyme Regis, Dorset, to take on the king and one of his finest commanders: Lord Feversham.
The king's royal army numbered about 2,600 men. They were professional troops and would have had the very best weapons at their disposal.

🛡 Aged 16, Monmouth got his first taste of fighting when he served in the fleet under his uncle, James Stuart – the same man that he fights here at Sedgemoor!

Rebels with a cause

Monmouth appealed to local men and soon volunteers flocked to help him in his cause against the king. With his right-hand men Lord Grey of Warke, as cavalry commander, and Nathaniel Wade heading up the infantry, Monmouth's army now totalled over 3,500. He had many more men with him to fight than the king but this wasn't necessarily going to guarantee him victory.

A soldier gives his true love a gift before going off to war.

Surprise attack

Monmouth actually thought that more men would come to help him and felt slightly disappointed at the low turn-out. He knew he would be facing a tough fight, especially as his troops weren't professional soldiers, but poor farmers and peasants who had never even seen a battle, let alone fought in one. So Monmouth decided to try something risky: a surprise night-time attack across the marshy bog of Sedgemoor.

Monmouth's men on the march.

Weapons

The favoured gun of the day was the flintlock musket – a reliable weapon that was always ready for use as it didn't have to be lit every time you wanted to fire it. It's doubtful that Monmouth's army would have had these 'state-of-the-art' guns, though.

This meant that they would have made do with matchlock muskets and the matches they kept having to light could be seen by the enemy, giving away their position.

Shhh!

This was a tactic that even the most experienced soldiers would find hard. Monmouth's rebels set off blindly into the night trying to keep quiet with their horses' hooves wrapped in rags, their cannon wheels well-oiled and orders to stab anyone who made a noise!

Enemy alert!

Even before any fighting had begun, their sneaky attack was foiled by a Royalist guard who spotted them creeping across Sedgemoor. He fired his pistol, galloped back to his camp and raised the alarm, yelling: "Beat your drums, the enemy is come. For the Lord's sake, beat your drums." What a catastrophe for Monmouth!

A Royalist soldier keeps a sharp eye out for lurking Jacobites.

Monmouth strikes

The actual fighting started very early the next morning. Monmouth felt desperate and worried about victory. He hoped that Feversham's men weren't ready to fight and so quickly sent his cavalry ahead, closely followed by his infantry. The camp was actually only 1,200 m away. Despite this, Grey still got lost.

No cover

He and his cavalry couldn't find the dry ditch that marked the best place to cross over into the enemy camp, though. They panicked and lost no time in fleeing from the battlefield, leaving the poor rebel infantry with no protective cover. What sissies!

Artillery men ready their cannons again after the first exchange.

A Jacobite soldier takes aim at his target and res. His musket is old-fashioned, though, and it will ake him valuable time to reload.

Firepower

The unprotected rebel infantry was no match for the skilled Royalists. They were well-equipped with what would have probably been the most technologically advanced weaponry of the day. They opened fire on Monmouth's men, slaughtering them with ease. Before long, the rebellion was all but over.

Rebel defeat

The bravest rebels stayed on to fight but most, including Monmouth himself, fled. When the sun rose, Feversham and his men crossed the ford and chased the remaining rebels until nearly all of them were killed or captured. Monmouth went into hiding, but after nine days of searching, the king's army caught him. They brought him back to London to face a beheading at Tower Hill.

Losses

The results of this battle show how important it is to have skilled men in your army. The inexperienced rebels lost over 1,000 men, with a further 500 captured. The Royalists, despite having a smaller army, had many more experienced soldiers and their losses probably totalled no more than 100 men.

Pitching in

The battle of Sedgemoor was also known as the 'Pitchfork Rebellion' because the rebel farm labourers used pitchforks as weapons.

The battle of Culloden

Date: 16 April 1746
Where: Culloden, near Inverness
Why: Stuarts trying to get the throne back
Armies: government army vs. Jacobite rebel army
Who won: government army

B y 1744 England was ruled by the unpopular German Hanoverians. The English people were unhappy with their rulers but across the English Channel, this state of affairs was all good news for the Stuarts in France...

A Stuart claim

The Stuarts were eager to get their hands back on the English throne and, with the English people unhappy at who was ruling their country, the time was ripe for an attack. So, Bonnie Prince Charlie (**WW**), of the Stuart dynasty took up the challenge to fight the Jacobite cause at Culloden – the last battle ever to be fought on British soil.

⚐ Prince Charles got his 'Bonnie' nickname because he was thought to be very handsome.

⚐ Supporters gather to help Bonnie Prince Charlie – but there aren't nearly enough men to take on the government's powerful army.

London or Scotland?

Charlie arrived on the north coast of Scotland in 1745 and moved southwards bit-by-bit, recruiting men as he went. By the time he reached Derby in December, he still hadn't got enough men for a good-sized army – perhaps people weren't as supportive of his cause after all... Charlie was worried:

should he still go to London with a far smaller army than expected or go back to Scotland? Following advice, Prince Charlie returned north.

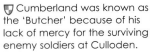 The Scots were fighting for the right to rule themselves.

Bad move

Returning to Scotland was the wrong decision, though, as Charlie was to find out. He should have gone with his gut instinct and headed for London, where this battle might have turned out better for him. Little did he know that Jacobite supporters in Wales and Oxfordshire were getting ready to fight for him and the Hanoverian king, George II, was about to flee from England to France. If Prince Charlie had gone to London, history might have been very different.

Jacobite toast

In 1702 William of Orange was thrown from his horse when it stumbled over a molehill. William died of his injuries and Jacobite supporters, hoping for a Stuart **succession**, secretly toasted the mole that caused his death by raising their glasses to 'The little gentleman in black velvet'!

Duke vs. Prince

The two armies eventually clashed at Culloden Moor in Scotland in the spring of the next year. It was William Augustus, the Duke of Cumberland, (**WW**) who led the government army against Charlie.

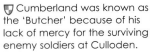 Cumberland was known as the 'Butcher' because of his lack of mercy for the surviving enemy soldiers at Culloden.

The men march until the early morning but still the enemy camps aren't in sight.

Surprise, surprise...?

The night before the battle, Charlie's men tried to launch a surprise attack on Cumberland's men. Even after marching until sunrise, however, the Jacobites weren't in sight of the government camps. What's more, half of the Prince's army had managed to get lost and Cumberland's men were already getting ready for the fight. There was no choice but to abandon the original plan and retreat.

What a walkover!

When Charlie's men finally met the enemy, it was a total walkover. They were hungry and exhausted. The government soldiers unleashed showers of gunfire at them and, with hardly any firepower of their own, there was little they could do.

The Scots charge into battle, shouting war cries to frighten the enemy.

Bang, bang

A few groups of brave rebel soldiers managed to dodge the bullets and charge into the government army but they did little damage. Nearly every man that tried was shot down before they even got near.

A few rebels try to offer covering fire to the charging infantry.

Charlie the coward

Charlie was a terrible soldier. He did little to help his men and, despite wanting to be king, he didn't want to get hurt in battle or die for his cause. As he watched his men fall, Charlie realised that the battle was lost and fled. Some leader!

All in an hour's work

In less than an hour the battle of Culloden was over and famously signalled the end of the Jacobite cause. Cumberland was the hero of the hour – he had stopped the rebels, kept the Stuarts from the throne and all with minimal casualties to his own army.

🛡 Soldiers clash in a bloody skirmish towards the end of the battle.

Remembering the dead

Cumberland ordered his men to kill all the Jacobites that they could – even if they were wounded. More important commanders were captured, tried and later executed. Today, visiting Culloden is a sobering event. Even though they challenged the king of England, the mass graves of the many Scottish **clansmen** that were killed that day are a very sad sight.

Charlie in love

When the Bonnie Prince fled, legend has it that he met a girl called Flora Macdonald (WW) who risked her life for him.

She smuggled Charlie to the Isle of Skye where his loyal supporters were waiting to take him to safety in France. Flora and Charlie fell in love and when he left she kept a lock of his hair as a keepsake. She was arrested and taken to the Tower of London for helping the prince but was eventually released.

Scottish battles

It's often said your worst enemy is the one that is closest to you. That's definitely true for Scotland and England. These two neighbouring countries have had a long history of fighting with one another – all for the lure of great power and riches!

Bad neighbours

When England ruled over Scotland, some Scots didn't mind. They even helped England fight against their own countrymen! Other people still wanted Scotland to be independent, though, and this led to many wars between the two countries.

Who should rule?

The warring situation was never fiercer than during the 13th and 14th centuries. At this time there were two people who wanted to be king of Scotland: Robert the Bruce, 5th Lord of Annandale, (WW) and John Balliol, Lord of Galloway.

🛡 Scottish soldiers in full battle dress.

Sneaky Edward

King Edward I of England was asked to help Scotland decide who would be the best ruler. Instead of helping, Edward saw this opportunity to try to control Scotland himself. He eventually chose Balliol to be king, mainly because he was weaker than Bruce and, therefore, easier to boss around. Little did Balliol know what he'd let himself in for...

🛡 Robert the Bruce – a hero of Scotland and one its greatest kings.

Call for help

Edward made demand after demand on Scotland and Balliol soon realised he was in trouble. He turned to France who, under a special treaty called the Auld Alliance, had to help. It wasn't long before Edward and England invaded Scotland and, despite help from France, as the end of the 13th century approached it looked like Scotland was all but beaten.

William Wallace was not a nobleman but a commoner.

Scottish soldiers gather ready to fight for their country.

Scottish crusaders

But not quite... There was still some fighting power left in Scotland. Revolts broke out against the English led by powerful guardians of Scotland such as William Wallace, above, and Robert the Bruce. These men were ready to die for the right for Scotland to be independent. What's more, they had loyal armies to back them up.

Edward II

When Edward I of England died, his son – Edward II (WW) – took over the fight for Scotland. It was this English king who met fearless Robert the Bruce on the battlefields at Bannockburn – one of the most important Scottish battles in history...

The Auld Alliance

Scotland, France and Norway made a treaty called the Auld Alliance. This special friendship, made in the 12th century, stated that if England invaded any of these countries, the other two would help defend them.
The treaty wasn't just about protection, though. It also allowed free trade between the countries, which was great for the Scottish as they loved French wine!

The battle of Bannockburn

Date: 24 June 1314
Where: Bannockburn, near Stirling
Why: power over Scotland
Armies: English vs. Scots
Who won: Scots

Bannockburn was one of the most important battles of the Scottish Wars of Independence. It was a fight between Robert the Bruce and Edward II for Stirling Castle – one of the last great Scottish strongholds still under English control at the time.

Besieged!

Robert's brother, Edward Bruce, held the castle in a deadly siege for many months, hoping to starve out the English inside. It didn't work, so he gave the English a deadline: either get reinforcements to improve your defence by Midsummer's Day or lose the castle!

Stirling Castle in Scotland where the siege took place.

Help arrives

The English did indeed send for more men – in the form of the king of England – Edward II! Edward brought with him a 25,000-strong army of professional knights that must have seemed daunting to the much smaller Scottish force of 9,000 untrained local volunteers.

This type of helmet, used at Bannockburn, is called a full helm and would have been very good at protecting a soldier's face.

Don't get comfy, Edward!

The confident king underestimated the fearsome Robert and his loyal army, though, and that was a big mistake… Robert's men were fired up and willing to sacrifice anything to get their freedom.

🛡 King Edward II is most famously remembered for being brutally murdered.

To war!

On the morning of the battle, while the English were still preparing, the Scots were ready and in position. Round one to Robert for being well organised! The Scots had practised hard for the battle and their first move was going to be a **schiltron** attack to stop the English heavy cavalry as it charged at their infantry.

🛡 Robert was leaving nothing to chance. He would have made sure that his men were awake and fully prepared.

Say a prayer

King Edward saw the Scottish army kneel down to pray and thought they were actually begging for his mercy. Typical Edward for thinking that he was braver than them. Again, he underestimated his enemy. Robert and his army were actually praying to God for a swift victory.

🛡 Robert's men bow their heads and pray for success.

Into battle

The battle commenced! Edward's cavalry advanced forward, crossing a steep **gorge** between the two armies. Robert's men were waiting for them, standing firm in solid schiltron formations.

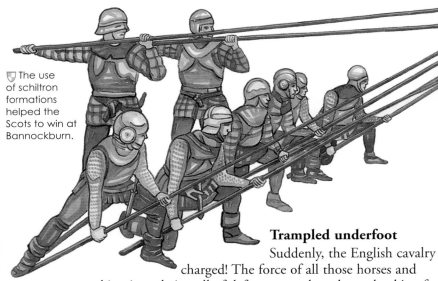

The use of schiltron formations helped the Scots to win at Bannockburn.

Trampled underfoot

Suddenly, the English cavalry charged! The force of all those horses and men smacking into their wall of defence must have been shocking for the Scottish soldiers, but they held fast killing many English knights with their long pikes, whilst others were hauled from their horses and trampled underfoot. Round two to Robert!

Watch out!

The English were in total confusion. More and more of their men had crossed the gorge and, on hearing an order to fire, started letting loose showers of arrows. But the order was a false one and the English archers hit their own men. Disaster!

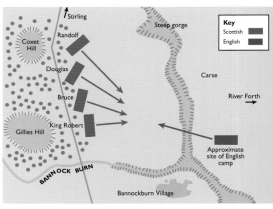

Key
Scottish
English

Stirling
Steep gorge
Randolf
Coxet Hill
Douglas
Carse
Bruce
River Forth
King Robert
Gillies Hill
Approximate site of English camp
BANNOCK BURN
Bannockburn Village

A map of the armies' movements.

Robert advances

By this time, both the king's cavalry and his archers were befuddled and scattered about the battlefield. Robert saw this as the sign he'd been waiting for. He and his men advanced like a massive wall in their schiltron formations, pushing the chaotic English into the gorge. Every time the English soldiers tried to charge back at them, they were pushed back again.

In the gorge

The sides of the gorge were steep and soon became a death-trap, slippery with muddy water and mushy bodies with no route of escape. English soldiers were being cut down left, right and centre. Horses and men were crushed together and the gorge became thick with dead bodies. Any English that did manage to cross the rivers were immediately run down by the Scots cavalry. It was totally hopeless – all was lost!

Standing ready for a charge with a sharp bill.

Victorious!

King Edward could see the battle was not going his way. With his head hung in shame, he made a quick exit back to the South, giving up Stirling to the Scots. The Scottish were victorious without a doubt and Robert the Bruce was a hero. He'd spent 18 years tirelessly fighting the cause for freedom and now he'd won.

Learn your lesson!

Bannockburn must have been a real lesson for Edward. Never again would he be so sure of a victory in battle. He still refused to recognise Robert the Bruce as King of Scotland, though. It was only after his death, when Edward III (WW) took the throne, that Robert was acknowledged as king.

The battle of Flodden

Date: 9 September 1513
Where: Branxton, Northumberland
Why: power over Scotland
Armies: English vs. Scots
Who won: English

It's 1513, Henry VIII (**WW**) is king and England is at war with France. Henry hasn't forgotten how pally the French and the Scots are, though, and gathers together a large army before he leaves for the war in France.

Henry VIII loved sport and gambling, and was an accomplished musician, author and poet.

Lucky decision

What a wise and lucky move for him that he did, as it wasn't long before the Scottish king, James IV (**WW**), got fed up with Henry's warring with France and assembled an army to cross over the Scottish border to England and to war!

Camp

King James set up camp on Flodden Hill – a great position from which he could survey the land below and, more importantly, the English army. Down below, under the charge of King Henry's ace commander, Thomas Howard (**WW**), the English troops prepared for battle.

James won't budge

Once in position, Howard sent a bold message to King James asking him to decamp from the hilltop and fight on the plain below. James wasn't stupid, though, and refused to move from his clever vantage point.

James IV was a popular king and helped unite the people of Scotland against England.

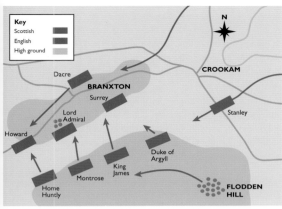

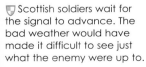 Flodden battlemap showing the movement of troops and the nobles in command.

It's raining again

The weather on the day of the battle was miserable: rain, rain and more rain. Trudging through the sludge of mud, Howard advanced on James' army. From the top of the hill, James could easily see the enemy troops but decided not to attack.

Smoke screen

He had spied another hill – Branxton Hill – that lay between him and the English. He knew that if the English captured it they would be in the same valuable position that the Scots were. So James ordered fires to be lit to create a wall of smoke between him and Howard's men. Hiding behind the smoke, the sneaky Scots decamped and made for Branxton.

Smart move

This decision to move was very important as all that stood between James and Howard now was flat land. The Scots definitely had the advantage: a steep slope to charge down and a great view of everything that was happening. The English troops must have been terrified as they huddled together at the bottom of a huge hill facing an enormous Scottish army glaring down.

Scottish soldiers wait for the signal to advance. The bad weather would have made it difficult to see just what the enemy were up to.

Henry VIII

Henry VIII was a great monarch. He loved having fun and spent much of his free time enjoying sports, games and music. He famously got married a total of six times in his attempts to produce a suitable heir for the English throne who would govern once he was dead. Three of his children went on to become great rulers themselves: Edward VI, Mary I and Elizabeth I. Henry left a lasting legacy for England: many castles and fortresses were built under his rule as well as a grand navy – the first in English history – which included the *Mary Rose*.

Let's fight!

The battle started, but not well for the Scots. First there was a deafening artillery exchange. The Scots had huge, heavy cannons which were difficult to move around. The English, however, had smaller, nippier ones which were easy to move and easier to reload, allowing them to shoot their foe with ease. James saw this carnage but wasn't disheartened. He ordered an almighty charge down the hill, resulting in the slaughter of countless English soldiers.

🛡 A 16th-century Scottish soldier would most likely wear a skullcap and a targe into battle. Some were more fortunate, having mail and helmets, others less so.

James IV coat of arms   Howard coat of arms

🛡 The Howard coat of arms, above, was given to Thomas Howard for his success at Flodden.

Charge!

Next, feeling confident, James charged down the hill himself with more men. The English must have been quaking in their boots as the king of Scotland sped towards them but they stood their ground and let loose arrows, killing Scots by the dozen.

The hill

With James and most of his men at the bottom of the hill, the English saw their chance: they clambered up the hill and attacked the small number of Scottish troops trying to defend it. The fierce Scots fought bravely but they were no match for their skilled English counterparts. Some Scots fled and others were slain where they stood. The fortunes of the English had changed: they had control of the top of the hill!

A typical Scottish suit of armour.

The battle is nearing its end and many men are dead.

Defeat

The English troops were better positioned by now, killing Scotsmen with relative ease. James and his loyal men fought on valiantly but were eventually forced to accept defeat.

A sad end

The result of this battle was a terrible loss for the Scottish, leaving over 10,000 Scotsmen killed or injured including many noblemen and, of course, King James himself.

St Mawes Castle in Cornwall was built under orders from Henry VIII to protect England from Spanish and French invaders.

The Hundred Years War

Date: 1337–1453
Where: mostly in France
Why: the right to the French throne
Armies: English allied army vs. French army
Who won: both sides at different times but the French finally won

One of the most important battles in English history wasn't just one battle, but a whole series of them: the Hundred Years War. Imagine a war lasting that long!

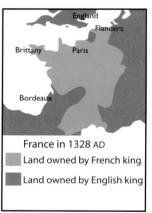

France in 1328 AD

Land owned by French king

Land owned by English king

France in 1430 AD

Land owned by French king

Land owned by English king

Land owned by
Duke of Burgandy

Conflict

The Hundred Years War actually lasted 116 years, and was a huge conflict between England and France for the right to the French throne.

The first map above shows how much of France the French king owned before the start of the Hundred Years War. As the war continued, you can see on the second map how the land ownership changed as the English king, and a chap called the Duke of Burgandy, conquered areas of the country.

One trade link that England enjoyed very much was being able to buy French wine.

Part 1: 1337–1360

At this time, England and France had trading links with each other. Through these links, England gained control of large areas of France and, as a result, French allies. This annoyed the French king no end and caused bitterness over trading. What's more, King Edward III had a claim to the French throne through marriage. These things were all leading to one thing: war!

Into battle

And what a war! In 1346 Edward invaded France leading to the first major battle of the Hundred Years conflicts: Crecy. Despite heavy fighting, and the fact that the French army was much larger than the English one, Edward used the skill of his archers and their ace longbows to the max. England was triumphant!

A workman making arrows for the many battles.

The Black Death

In 1348, however, the **Black Death** put a stop to war. England was hit hard and the king had neither the funds nor the enthusiasm to go back to war. But once the Black Death had passed, war was definitely back on the menu!

Rats were the cause of the Black Death, spreading disease through the land.

Victory

In 1356 the English won another great battle at Poitiers under the expert lead of Edward III's son, Edward, Prince of Wales – also known as the Black Prince. Again the English were outnumbered and again it was the might of the skilled English archers who stole victory for England.

Artwork depicting the Battle of Sluys in 1340 – a sea conflict during the Hundred Years War.

End of chivalry

Historians believe that the battle of Crecy marked the end of the age of chivalry. Chivalry was of the highest importance before this. For example, the Black Prince got his name because, when fighting, he dressed in black in honour of his ladies. But even though people believed that war should be conducted in a very courteous manner, it didn't always guarantee victory. New armies and new tactics showed that 'fighting dirty' got more results.

Edward, the Black Prince, had military talent and was very successful at battles such as Crecy and Poitiers. He was a big fan of the English longbow.

Part 2: 1360–1400

Next, a period of peace came and King Edward got the lands that he wanted. Had the English won the struggle for the French throne? No way, José! Charles V became king of France and he wasn't about to let his beloved country come under English rule. Over the next few years he seized back all the French land that England had been given and called a truce.

A big change

This period of conflict saw many changes in the way that countries fought one another. New weapons weren't just given to the nobility anymore. Peasants were also now properly equipped, meaning that they could fight more efficiently, gaining power, notoriety and the rewards that were once reserved

for the aristocracy. Countries had permanent armies, giving monarchs new power and constant defence from attacks – both abroad and at home.

Part 3: 1400–1422

But when Henry V came to power, the war started again. He invaded France in 1415 and challenged the French at the famous battle of Agincourt. Once again, the French way outnumbered the English but this didn't deter Henry.

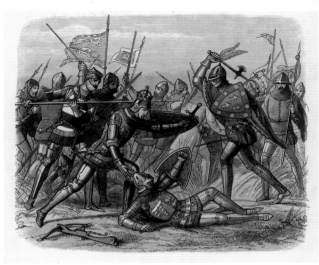

⬆ Henry V was a dynamic monarch and managed to unify the crowns of England and France – that was some achievement!

⬆ Agincourt was a great success for the English, but Henry never wanted to fight there. It was only when he was forced into a corner that he met the French in battle at this famous site.

England scores again!

Henry's expert archers made mincemeat of the enemy and many Frenchmen in their heavy armour – the English side had much lighter armour – got too tired to fight. They fell to the ground in the battle scrum and suffocated in the thick, gloopy mud. It was an eye-goggling victory for England. In the three hours that the battle lasted for, the English claimed an amazing 10,000 French lives. Their losses were a mere 200. After Agincourt Henry went on to gain control of Normandy and make further alliances throughout France.

Part 4: 1422–1453

By 1428 England was ready to fight France again for more land. But as the years passed, English alliances in France began to disappear and the French captured back more and more land until, in 1453 at the battle of Castillon, the English were totally crushed and the Hundred Years War was finally at an end. Phew!

Where next?

I f you enjoyed learning about the many different battles in this book, the best way to find out more about them is to visit the battlesites, surf the web or go to a re-enactment day.

Visitor centres

Many battlesites have good visitor centres with lots of background information on the people involved in the fighting, what changes the battles had on the land around them, and results of archaeological digs that might have been carried out, for example.

Surf the web

English Heritage has done much research into the major fields of conflict in England. Visit their website to find out more at www.english-heritage.org.uk. Whilst online, why not check out these sites, too:

www.battlefieldstrust.com
www.battleofshrewsbury.org
www.tewkesbury.org.uk/battlefield
www.nts.org.uk (Scottish battles)
www.undiscoveredscotland.co.uk
www.scotclans.com (Scottish battles)

NOTE
The above web addresses are correct at the time of going to print. English Heritage has no control over the content of any of the above sites other than its own.

Re-enactment days

Another fun way to learn more about battles is to go to a re-enactment day, where people dress up as soldiers from the past and act out famous battles. You get the chance to see, smell and hear what a real battle might have been like: the war cries, the smell of gunpowder and the boom of a cannon. English Heritage regularly holds these sorts of events, including the 'Festival of History' which is held every year at different country houses. See the website for more details.

The Battlefields Trust

The Battlefields Trust is a valuable organisation that aims to preserve battlesites in England, educating the public about the conflicts that have taken place in this country. It is important that we remember the men and women who fought in the past and helped to shape the country that we live in today. Yes, some were fighting for land and money, but others were fighting for freedom –

and that's far more important. Visit the Trust's website (*see* page 98) to find out more about their work and the fields of conflict that they support.

Glossary

These words can be found in bold in the text.

archaeologists
Experts who study the past by finding and analysing artefacts and human remains, for example.

artillery
Any machine, such as a cannon or musket, used to fire something during a battle.

besieged
When a building or town is blocked in by an enemy to make them surrender.

the Black Death
A terrible disease that started in the 14th century and spread across England and Europe, killing thousands of people. Also known as the Black Plague.

camaraderie
Friendship and a general feeling of happiness.

causeway
Road or pathway over water that attaches two pieces of land together.

cavalry
Soldiers who fight on horses.

chivalry
The institution of knighthood and knightly virtues.

civil war
When people from the same country fight one another.

clansmen
People who belong to a clan – a group of people who have the same ancestors.

counter-attacked
A defensive attack that a king or commander might do once he has been attacked himself.

Dark Ages
A period of time before the Romans conquered England.

dissolved
Got rid of.

dragoons
A soldier trained to fight on foot but who uses a horse to get from place to place.

dynasty
A family that has a lot of power, usually political.

Ealdormann
A Saxon nobleman.

exchange
When two armies fire at each other at the same time, e.g. an exchange of cannons.

flank
The men who stand at the sides of the army when it's in formation.

gorge
A deep ditch.

hearth-troop
Some of the best soldiers in an army who were very well-equipped with weapons and who usually fought close to the king to keep him protected.

hilt
The handle of a sword.

House of Lancaster
A dynasty of English kings descended from John of Gaunt, Duke of Lancaster.

House of York
A dynasty of English kings descended from Richard, Duke of York.

infantry
Soldiers who fight on foot.

Ironsides
A troop formed by Oliver Cromwell who were considered to be the best soldiers in the New Model Army. They were very disciplined and showed the more unruly men how to behave and fight like professional soldiers.

joust
A pretend fight between two knights.

Lancastrians
People who belong to the House of Lancaster.

Lord Protector
A person in charge of ruling a country who isn't a king or queen.

medieval
Refers to anything from the Middle Ages.

Middle Ages
A period of time from about the 11th century to the 15th century.

mints
Buildings where treasure, gold and money are stored.

monarch
A king or a queen who rules a country.

nobility
Someone born into a noble family, such as a king, a princess or a duke.

overthrew
Got rid of.

Parliament
A body of politicians. Comes from the French word 'parler' which means to talk.

rebel
A person who refuses to accept authority, such as that of a king or a Parliament.

schiltron
A group of men who crouch shoulder-to-shoulder under or behind their shields while they hold their pikes out toward the enemy.

shieldwall
A great military tactic where men stand tightly packed together, holding their shields in an overlapping pattern. This means that each soldier is protected by both his own shield and that of his neighbour.

stronghold
A building that's strongly defended with soldiers and good fortifications, for example.

succession
How a king or an MP comes to power.

Tudors
People from the House of Tudor, a family who ruled in the 15th, 16th and 17th centuries.

Yorkists
People who belong to the House of York.

Index

Picture acknowledgements

Every effort has been made to credit pictures accurately.

All illustrations © Fiona Powers 2005 except 13b, 28t, 31b, 35b, 42m, 52m, 72b, 83b, 94b

Photographs:
5, 6t, 7t&b, 19, 20t, 20/21b, 23t&m, 24t, 25t, 26b, 27m, 28b, 30m&b, 32t, 39t&m, 41m, 42, 54b, 57b, 58t, 61, 62t&m, 63, 64b, 65t&m, 66t&m, 67t&b, 69b, 71t, 72t&b, 77b, 78b, 81, 82, 92t, 98t&b, 99t © English Heritage Special Events Dept.
4, 16b, 24m, 51b, 52, 55b, 70t, 95t, 99b © English Heritage Special Events Dept./Neil Holmes
27m © English Heritage Special Events Dept./PL Isemonger
22b, 25t © English Heritage Special Events Dept./Dick Clarke

10tl, 11l, 39b, 54m, 55t, 64t, 68t&b, 73t&b, 74t © English Heritage/NMR

10bl, 11l, 22t, 25b, 70b, 93tr © English Heritage Photo Library
22t, 32b, 33m, 54t © English Heritage Photo Library/Jonathan Bailey
60b © English Heritage Photo Library/Paul Highnam

10t&b, 14b, 18, 20m, 21m, 28t, 31, 35t, 51t&m, 59, 67m, 69m, 71b, © G Foard/Battlefields Trust
9b © S Barker/Battlefields Trust
58b © D Beaumont/Battlefields Trust

6b, 12b, 15t&m, 38b, 41t&b, 56, 58m, 62b, 65t&b, 66m, 69t, 86b, 89 © Ken and Denise Guest

43b, 49, 50b, 53b, 75b, 79t, 81t, 82m © Geoff Buxton

9t, 27b, 33t, 35m, 37t&b, 45t, 46b, 47t&b, 48t, 50t © Clive Hawkins

80b, 82t, 83, 84t, 85t&b, 87t&b, 91, 92m, 93tl © Ian Deveney

74b, 77t, 78t © The National Trust for Scotland

75t, 80t, 90, 95b, 96t, 97t&b © Mary Evans Picture Library

81b © Courtesy of the Director, National Army Museum

15b, 16t, 21m © The Vikings Photographs/Steve Reeve, Ferry View Photography.
email: photography@ferryview5.freeserve.co.uk

21t © The Vikings/Ian Muirhead

30t, 35m, 38t, 43 © Mark Arnold

29b, 97b © The Archers of Ravenwood

53t © The British Library

45b © Kirsten Wright 2005

46t © Denyer

66b © Northampton County Council

86t © Crown copyright reproduced courtesy of Historic Scotland

33b, 84b © National Portrait Gallery, London

23b © Copyright Reading Museum Service (Reading Borough Council). All rights reserved.

48b © From the Picture Collection, Royal Holloway, Univ. of London